DAILY HE LEADS ME

Daily He Leads Me

Hannah Whitall Smith

*Selected and Adapted
by Ann Spangler*

VINE
BOOKS

Servant Publications
Ann Arbor, Michigan

Cover photo © H. Armstrong Roberts
Book design by John B. Leidy

Vine Books is an imprint of Servant Publications
designed to serve Evangelical Christians.

Published by Servant Books
P.O. Box 8617,
Ann Arbor, Michigan 48107

The scripture quotations in this publication are from the
Revised Standard Version of the Bible, copyrighted 1946,
1952 © 1971, 1973 by the Division of Christian Education of
the National Council of the Churches of Christ in the U.S.A.,
and used by permission.

Printed in the United States of America
ISBN 0-89283-228-2

85 86 87 88   10 9 8 7 6 5 4 3 2 1

Preface

HANNAH WHITALL SMITH was born in Philadelphia in 1832, just five years before Victoria began her sixty-four-year reign as monarch of England. She died in 1911, three years shy of World War I. During her seventy-nine years, Hannah Smith witnessed the transformation of life wrought by the industrial revolution, the bloody strife of civil war in America, and the social revolution generated by the women's movement of the late nineteenth and early twentieth century.

Never one to stand on the sidelines, she engaged in the debates of the day with relish. She and her husband Robert were active in evangelical movements in the United States and Britain and became well-known preachers on both sides of the Atlantic. At their home in England, dubbed Friday's Hill, they entertained such notable figures as George Bernard Shaw, Bertrand Russell, Oscar Wilde, Beatrice and Sidney Webb, and Bernard Berenson.

Hannah's spiritual heritage, though rooted in her Quaker upbringing, was shaped primarily by her belief that the Bible held the words of eternity. Buffeted by life's tragedies, which included the death of four out of seven of her children, she consistently turned to scripture for answers to questions about life and its meaning. The results of her own steady faith and confidence in the word of God are graciously expressed in her best-selling book, *The Christian's Secret of a Happy Life*. They are also contained in lesser-known books, such as *The Open*

Secret, Every Day Religion, The God of All Comfort, and *Bible Readings.*

It is from these latter sources that I have compiled *Daily He Leads Me.* I have tried to draw from her writings reflections which most clearly convey her understanding of scriptural truths. Often I simply extracted the scripture passage and the reflections directly from her text. Occasionally, I have supplied the scripture passage at the head of the daily readings. Throughout the editing I have attempted to respect Hannah Smith's style and tone, to say things the way she would have and to change words only where the meaning was obscure or the language quaint.

Many of the themes—confidence in the love of God, abandonment to the will of God, knowledge of the character of God—come up again and again, as they must have in her own life. I have not been overly concerned about repetition, since the book is best used as a daily guide, in which each selection is allowed to instruct and inspire one day at a time. As in most things, we learn best when we learn life's lessons more than once.

My hope for readers is that their own spiritual life and understanding will be enriched, as mine has been, by the insights of this remarkable Christian, distinguished by her faith in an all-loving, all-powerful God, and confident in his care, no matter what the circumstances.

I owe special thanks to Vickie Wozny for her generosity in offering me her home for a full week of quiet and concentrated work on the book. Without her offer, the work of compiling and editing would have been much more laborious and less of the real pleasure that it turned out to be.

ANN SPANGLER

January

1 *See what love the Father has given us, that we should be called children of God; and so we are.* (1 Jn 3:1)

The love that God gives to us is the love a father has for his son, a tender protecting love, that knows our weakness and our need, and cares for us accordingly. He treats us as sons, and all he asks in return is that we treat him as a father, whom we can trust without anxiety. We must take the son's place of dependence and trust, and must let him do the father's part. Too often we take upon our own shoulders the father's part, and try to take care of and provide for ourselves. But no good earthly father would want his children to take upon their young shoulders the burden of his duties. Much less would our Heavenly Father want to lay upon us the burden of his.

2 *Do not fear or be dismayed: take all the fighting men with you, and arise, go up to Ai; see, I have given into your hand the king, and his people, his city, and his land.* (Jos 8:1)

Nothing is more abundantly proved in the Bible than this, that the Lord will fight for us, if we will only let him. He knows that we have no strength or might against our spiritual enemies;

and, like a tender mother, when her helpless children are attacked by an enemy, he fights for us. All he asks is that we be still and let him. This is the only sort of spiritual conflict that is ever successful.

But, you may ask, are we not to do any fighting ourselves? Of course we are to fight, but not in this fashion. We are to fight the "good fight of faith," as Paul exhorted Timothy; and the fight of faith is not a fight of effort or of struggle, but it is a fight of trusting. It is the kind of fight that Hezekiah fought when he and his army marched out to meet their enemy, singing songs of victory as they went, and finding their enemy all dead bodies. Our part in this fight is to hand the battle over to the Lord and to trust him for the victory.

3 *Stand therefore, having girded your loins with truth, and having put on the breastplate of righteousness, and having shod your feet with the equipment of the gospel of peace; besides all these, taking the shield of faith, with which you can quench all the flaming darts of the evil one.* (Eph 6:14-16)

We are to put on God's armor, not our own. The apostle tells us what it is. It is the girdle of truth, and the breastplate of righteousness, and the preparation of the gospel of peace on our feet, and the shield of faith to quench the flaming darts of the evil one.

There is nothing here about promises or resolutions; nothing about hours and days of agonizing struggles, and of bitter remorse. "Besides all these, taking the shield of faith." Faith is the one essential thing, without which all else is useless. We must not only hand the battle over to the Lord, but we must leave it with him, and must have absolute faith that he will conquer. It is here where the fight comes in. It seems so unsafe to sit still and do nothing but trust the Lord. The temptation to take the battle back into our own hands is often tremendous. To keep hands off in spiritual matters is as hard for us as it is for the drowning man to keep hands off the one who is trying to rescue him. We all know how impossible it is to rescue a drowning man who tries to help his rescuer, and it is equally impossible for the Lord to fight our battles for us when we insist upon trying to fight them ourselves. It is not that he will not, but that he cannot. Our interference hinders his working.

4 *My grace is sufficient for you, for my power is made perfect in weakness.* (2 Cor 12:9)

Our Lord tells us that without him we can do nothing, but do we really believe him? In spite of all our failures, we cannot help thinking that, if only we should try harder and be more persistent, we should be equal to any encounter. But we entirely overlook the vital fact that our natural powers are of no avail in spiritual regions or with spiritual enemies. The grub of the dragonfly that lives at the bottom of the pond may be a finely developed and vigorous grub; but, when it becomes a dragonfly, the powers of its grub life that availed for creeping about in the mud would be useless for winging its flight in the free air.

Just as our skill in walking on the earth would avail us nothing if we had to fly in the air, so our natural powers are of no avail in spiritual warfare. In fact, if we try to depend on them, they are real hindrances. Trusting in ourselves, when dealing with our spiritual enemies, not only causes failure, but in the end it causes rebellion; and a great deal of what is called "spiritual conflict" might far better be named "spiritual rebellion." God has told us to cease from our own efforts, and to hand our battles over to him, and we point blank refuse to obey him. We fight, it is true, but it is not a fight of faith, but a fight of unbelief. Our spiritual "wrestling," of which we are often so proud, is really a wrestling, not for God against his enemies, but against him on the side of his enemies. We allow ourselves to indulge in doubts and fears, and as a consequence we are plunged into darkness, and turmoil, and wrestlings of spirit. The single word that explains our dilemma is the word "unbelief," and the simple remedy is to be found in the word "faith."

5 *A man wrestled with him until the breaking of the day. When the man saw that he did not prevail against Jacob, he touched the hollow of his thigh; and Jacob's thigh was put out of joint as he wrestled with him.* (Gn 32:24-28)

You may wonder whether Jacob did not win victory by wrestling. To this I reply, that on the contrary, he gained his victory by being made so weak that he could not wrestle any longer. It was not Jacob who wrestled with the angel, but the angel who wrestled with Jacob. Jacob was the one to be overcome; and when the angel found that Jacob's resistance was so great that he could not "prevail against him," he was obliged to lame him, by putting his thigh out of joint; and then the victory was won. As soon as Jacob was too weak to resist any longer, he prevailed with God. He gained power when he lost it. He conquered when he could no longer fight.

Jacob's experience is ours. The Lord wrestles with us in order to bring us to a place of entire dependence on him. We resist as long as we have any strength; until at last he is forced to bring us to a place of helplessness, where we are obliged to yield; and then we conquer by this very yielding. Our victory is always the victory of weakness.

6 *Then Gideon perceived that he was the angel of the Lord. ... But the Lord said to him, "Peace be to you; do not fear, you shall not die."* (Jgs 6:22-23)

The Lord called Gideon for a work he felt he was incapable of accomplishing. But the Lord promised him victory, and peace. Then Gideon believed the Lord. Although the battle had not yet been fought, and no victories had been won, with the eye of faith he saw peace already secured. And he built an altar to the Lord, and called it *Jehovah-shalom*, i.e., "the Lord our Peace."

Of all the needs of the human heart none is greater than the need for peace; and none is more abundantly promised in the gospel. "Peace I leave with you," says our Lord, "My peace I give to you. Let not your heart be troubled, neither let it be afraid."

Our idea of peace is that it must be outward before it can be inward, that all enemies must be driven away and all troubles cease. But the Lord's idea is of an interior peace that can exist in the midst of turmoil, and can triumph over it. The ground of this sort of peace is found in the fact, not that we have overcome the world, or that we ever can, but that Christ has overcome it. Only the conqueror can proclaim peace, and the people, whose battles he has fought, can do nothing but enter into it. They can neither make nor unmake it. But, if they choose, they can refuse to believe in it, and so can fail to let it reign in their hearts. You may be afraid to believe that Christ has made peace for you, and so may live on in a weary state of warfare; but nevertheless he has done it.

7 *Have no anxiety about anything but in everything by prayer and supplication with thanksgiving let your requests be made known to God. And the peace of God, which passes all understanding, will keep your hearts and your minds in Christ Jesus. (Phil 4:6-7)*

The Bible tells us that Christ is our peace, and consequently, whether I feel as if I have peace or not, peace is really mine in Christ, and I must take possession of it by faith.

Practically I believe we can always enter into peace by a simple obedience to the command in Philippians. The steps here are very plain, and they are only two. First give up all anxiety, and second, hand over your cares to God; and then stand steadfastly and peace must come. It simply must, for there is no room for anything else.

8 *Behold, the days are coming, says the Lord, when I will raise up for David a righteous Branch, and he shall reign as king and deal wisely.... And this is the name by which he will be called: "The Lord is our righteousness." (Jer 23:5-6)*

Greater than any other need is our need of righteousness. Most of the struggles and conflicts of our Christian life come from our fights with sin and our efforts after righteousness. And I need not say how great are our failures. As long as we try to conquer sin or attain righteousness by our own efforts, we are bound to fail. But if we discover that the Lord is our righteousness, we will have got hold of a secret of victory. In the Lord Jesus Christ we have a fuller revelation of this wonderful name of God.

Experimentally it seems to me like this. We are not to try to have a stock of righteousness laid up in ourselves, from which to draw a supply when needed. Instead, we are to draw continual fresh supplies as we need them from the righteousness that is laid up for us in Christ. I mean, that if we need righteousness of any sort, such as patience, or humility, or love, it is useless for us to look within, hoping to find a supply there, for we never will find it; but we must simply take it by faith, as a possession that is stored up for us in Christ, who is our righteousness. If I cannot tell theologically how this is done, I know experimentally that it can be done and that the results are triumphant. I have seen sweetness and gentleness poured like a flood of sunshine into dark and bitter spirits, when the hand of faith has been reached out to grasp them as a present possession, stored up for all who need in Christ. I have seen sharp tongues made tender, anxious hearts made calm, and fretful spirits made quiet, by the simple step of taking by faith the righteousness that is ours in Christ.

9 *For he will give his angels charge of you / to guard you in all your ways. / On their hands they will bear you up, / lest you dash your foot against a stone.* (Ps 91:11-12)

The Lord is like a mother who holds the hand of her little child as they walk together, that she may keep it from falling over the snares that lie in its way. It is the mother holding the child that makes it safe, not the child holding the mother. Notice the words "bear you up," illustrated by the infant in the mother's arms, safe because of her upholding. Its little frightened gasps when danger is near, do not make it any safer, for its safety consists in the fact that its mother holds it, and everything depends on whether *she* is able to keep it safe.

10 *O taste and see that the Lord is good! / Happy is the man who takes refuge in him! (Ps 34:8)*

What does it mean to be good? What is it but to live up to the best and highest that one knows? Being good is exactly the opposite of being bad. To be bad is to know the right and not do it, but to be good is to do the best we know. Since God is omniscient, he must know what is the best and highest good of all, and therefore his goodness must necessarily be beyond question. I can never express what this knowledge meant to me. I had such a view of the real, actual goodness of God that I realized that nothing could possibly go wrong under his care, and it seemed to me that no one could ever be anxious again. Since then, when appearances have been against him, and when I have been tempted to question whether he has been unkind, neglectful, or indifferent, I have been brought up short by the words, "The Lord is good!"

11 *They spoke against God, saying, / "Can God spread a table in the wilderness?" (Ps 78:19)*

This seemed a very innocent question to ask. But God had promised to supply all the Israelites' needs in the wilderness. To ask this question betrayed a secret want of confidence in God's ability to do as he has promised. In spite of its innocent appearance, it was a real "speaking against" God. A good God could not have led his people into the wilderness and then have failed to "spread a table" for them. To question whether he was able to do it was to imply that he was not good. In the same way we are sometimes sorely tempted to ask a similar question. Circumstances often seem to make it so impossible for God to supply our needs, that we find ourselves over and over tempted to "speak against" him by asking if he can. Often as he has done it before, we seem unable to believe he can do it again, and in our hearts we limit him, because we do not believe his word nor trust his goodness.

12 All things were made through him, and without him was not anything made that was made. (Jn 1:3)

Few of us have not been tempted at one time or other to ask God why he has made us the way we are, with our own personal makeup. We do not like our peculiar temperaments or our special characteristics, and we long to be like someone else, who seems to have greater gifts of appearance or talent.

I remember a time in my life when I was tempted to be very rebellious about my own makeup. I was a plain-spoken, energetic sort of person, trying to be a good Christian, but with no special air of piety about me. But my sister was so saintly in her looks and had such a pious manner, that she seemed to be the embodiment of holiness. I felt sure I could be a great deal better Christian if only I could become like her in looks and manner. But all my struggles were useless. My natural temperament was far too energetic and outspoken for any appearance of saintliness, and many a time I said upbraidingly in my heart to God, "Why have you made me like this?" One day I came across a sentence in an old book that seemed to open my eyes: "Be content to be what thy God has made thee." It flashed on me that it really was a fact that God had made me, and that he must know the sort of creature he wanted me to be. If he had made me a potato plant, I must be satisfied to grow potatoes and not try to be a rose bush to grow roses. If he had fashioned me for humble tasks, I must be content to let others do the grander work. We are "God's workmanship," and God is good, therefore his workmanship must be good also. We may trust that he will make us something that will be to his glory, no matter how unlike this we may as yet feel ourselves to be.

13 Let the redeemed of the Lord say so, / whom he has redeemed from trouble and gathered in from the lands. (Ps 107:2)

We must join our voices to that of the psalmist. Our God is indeed a good God. But we must not say it with our lips only but with our whole being, with thought, word, and action, so that people will see we really mean it and will be convinced that it is a tremendous fact.

A great many things in God's divine providence do not look like goodness to the eye of sense, and in reading the Psalms we may wonder how the psalmist could say, after some of the things he records, "his mercy endures forever." But faith bows down before mysteries such as these and says, "The Lord is good, therefore all that he does must be good, no matter how it looks, and I can wait for his explanations."

A housekeeping illustration has often helped me here. If I have a friend whom I know to be a good housekeeper, I don't trouble over the fact that at house-cleaning time things in her house may seem to be more or less upset: carpets up, and furniture shrouded in coverings, and even perhaps painting and decorating, making some rooms uninhabitable. I say to myself, "My friend is a good housekeeper, and although things look so uncomfortable now, all this uproar is only because she means in the end to make it far more comfortable than it was before." This world is God's housekeeping; and although things at present look grievously upset, we know that he is good and therefore must be a good Housekeeper. We must be perfectly sure that all this present upset is only to bring about in the end a far better state of things than could have been possible without it. I dare say we have all felt at times as though we could have done God's housekeeping better than he does it himself, but, when we realize that God is good, we can feel this no longer.

14 *These all died in faith, not having received what was promised, but having seen it and greeted it from afar, and having acknowledged that they were strangers and exiles on earth. For people who speak thus make it clear that they are seeking a homeland.* (Heb 11:13-14)

We, too, are seeking a homeland. In other words, we are a *developing* race. It is not a *place* we are seeking, but a *condition*, a new nature and a new sphere of life. There are two *men* in the Bible: man as an animal and man as a spiritual being. Our natural man, the flesh man, or as the Bible calls it, the "old man," can never fulfill the righteousness of God, for it is of the earth, earthy. With our "sinful nature," the flesh, we must of necessity always serve the "law of sin." It is only the spiritual man, the man born of God, the resurrection man, who can mind the things of the Spirit; and, in fact, it is only such who can even *understand* God and his ways.

15 *Truly, truly, I say to you, unless a grain of wheat falls into the earth and dies, it remains alone; but if it dies, it bears much fruit.* (Jn 12:24)

A deeply taught Christian was asked by a despairing child of God, "Doesn't the world look to you like a wreck?" "Yes," was the reply, in a tone of cheerful confidence, "Yes, like the wreck of a bursting seed."

Any of us who have watched the first sprouting of an oak tree from the heart of a decaying acorn will understand what this means. Before the acorn can bring forth the oak, it must become itself a wreck. No plant ever came from any but a wrecked seed.

Our Lord uses this fact to teach us the meaning of his processes with us. The whole explanation of the apparent wreckage of the world at large, or of our own personal lives in particular, is here set forth. Looked at in this light, we can understand how it is that the Lord can be good, and yet can permit the existence of sorrow and wrong in the world he has created and in the lives of the human beings he loves.

It is his very goodness that compels him to permit it. For he knows that, only through such apparent wreckage, can the fruition of his glorious purposes for us be brought to pass. If we understand his ways, we, whose hearts also long for that fruition, will be able to praise him for all his goodness, even when things seem hardest and most mysterious.

16 *Lord, thou hast been our dwelling place in all generations.* (Ps 90:1)

The comfort or discomfort of our outward lives depends more upon the dwelling place of our bodies than upon almost any other material thing; and the comfort or discomfort of our inward life depends similarly upon the dwelling place of our souls.

Our dwelling place is the place where we live, not the place we merely visit. It is our home. All the interests of our earthly lives are bound up in our homes; and we do all we can to make them attractive and comfortable. But our souls need a comfortable dwelling place even more than our bodies; for inward comfort, as we all know, is of far greater importance than outward. Where the soul is full of peace and joy, outward surroundings are of comparatively little account.

It is of vital importance, then, that we should find out definitely where our souls are living. The Lord declares that he has been our dwelling place in all generations, but the question is: are we living in our dwelling place? The psalmist says of the children of Israel that they wandered in the wilderness, finding no city to dwell in. Hungry and thirsty, their souls fainted within them.

The truth is, our souls are made for God. He is our natural home, and we can never be at rest anywhere else. We always shall hunger and faint for the courts of the Lord, as long as we fail to take up our abode there.

17 *Because you have made the Lord your refuge, / the Most High your habitation, no evil shall befall you, / no scourge come near your tent.* (Ps 91:9-10)

How safe the psalmist declares this divine dwelling place to be! Notice how he says that we who are in this dwelling place shall be afraid of nothing: not the terror by night, nor the arrow by day, nor the plague that walks in darkness. Thousands shall fall beside us and around us, but no evil shall befall the soul that is hidden in this divine dwelling place.

All the terrors and all the plagues that have made our religious lives so wretched are included here, and from all of them we shall be delivered, if we make the Lord our habitation. This does not mean that we shall have no outward trials. Plagues in abundance may attack us, but nothing can come near our soul while we are dwelling in God.

A large part of the pain of life comes from the haunting "fear of evil" which so often besets us. Our lives are full of "supposes." Suppose this should happen, or suppose that should happen; what could we do; how could we bear it? But, if we are dwelling with God, all these supposes will drop out of our lives. Even when walking through the valley of the shadow of death, the psalmist could say, "I will fear no evil." If we are dwelling in God, we can say so too.

18 *Lead thou me to the rock that is higher than I;/for thou art my refuge,/ a strong tower against the enemy.*

(Ps 61:2-3)

He who cares for the sparrows and numbers the hairs of our head cannot possibly fail us. He is an impregnable fortress, into which no evil can enter and no enemy penetrate. I hold it, therefore, as a self-evident truth that the moment I have really committed anything into this divine dwelling place; all fear and anxiety should cease. While I keep anything in my own care, I may well fear and tremble, for it is indeed to the last degree unsafe. But in God's care, no security could be more absolute.

The only point is to run into this strong tower and stay there forever. It would be the height of folly, when the enemy was surrounding us on every side, to stand outside of a fortress and cry out for safety. If I want to be safe, *I must go in.*

19 *Let me dwell in thy tent for ever!/Oh to be safe under the shelter of thy wings!/For thou, O God, hast heard my vows,/thou hast given me the heritage of those who fear thy name.* (Ps 61:4-5)

The psalmist wants to dwell in the tent of God forever, to be safe under the shelter of God's wings. We must do the same. This dwelling forever in God's tent is sometimes very hard. It is comparatively easy to take a step of faith, but it is a far more difficult thing to abide steadfastly in the place into which we have stepped. A great many people dwell in God's fortress on Sunday and come out of it again as soon as Monday morning dawns. This is the height of folly. One cannot imagine any sensible refugee running into a fortress one day and the next day running out among the enemy again. We would think such a person had suddenly lost all his senses. But is it not even more foolish when it comes to the soul? Are our enemies any less active on Mondays than they are on Sundays, or are we any better able to cope with them when we are in bed than when we were kneeling at our prayers?

20 *He who dwells in the shelter of the Most High, / who abides in the shadow of the Almighty, / will say to the Lord, "My refuge and my fortress; / my God, in whom I trust."*
(Ps 91:1-2)

Abiding and trusting mean exactly the same thing. While I trust the Lord, I am abiding in him. If I trust him steadfastly, I am abiding in him steadfastly; if I trust him intermittently, I am running into him and running out again. I used to think there was some mystery about abiding in Christ, but I see now that it only means trusting him fully. When once you understand this, it becomes really the simplest matter in the world. We sometimes say, speaking of two human beings, that they "live in each other's hearts," and we simply mean that perfect love and confidence exist between them, and that doubts of one another are impossible. If my trust in the fortress of the Lord is absolute, I am abiding in the fortress; and this is the whole story.

21 *The name of the Lord is a strong tower; / the righteous man runs into it and is safe.* (Prv 18:10)

Since the Lord is our strong tower, nothing can possibly come to any harm that is committed to his care. As long as we believe this, our affairs remain in his care; the moment we begin to doubt, we take our affairs into our own hands, and they are no longer in the divine fortress. Things cannot be in two places at once. If they are in our own care, they cannot be in God's care, and if they are in God's care, they cannot be in our own. This is as clear as daylight, and yet, for the want of a little common-sense, people often get mixed up over it. They put their affairs into God's fortress and at the same time put them into their own fortress as well. Then they wonder why they are not taken care of. This is all folly. Either trust the Lord out and out, or else trust yourself out and out; but do not try to mix the two trusts, for they will not mix.

22 *Lord, thou hast been our dwelling place in all generations.* (Ps 90:1)

When we move into a new house, we not only move in ourselves, but we take with us all our belongings of every sort and description. Above all, we take our family. No one would be so foolish as to leave anything they cared for or anyone they loved outside. But I am afraid there are some of God's children who move into the dwelling place of God themselves, but by lack of faith leave their loved ones outside. More often than not it is their children who are so abandoned. We should be horrified at a father who in a time of danger should flee into a fortress for safety, but should leave his children outside; and yet hundreds of Christians do this very thing. Every anxious thought which we indulge about our children, proves that we have not really taken them with us into the dwelling place of God.

What I mean is this, that, if we trust for ourselves, we must trust for our loved ones also, especially our children. God is more truly their Father than their earthly fathers are. If they are dear to us, they are far dearer to him. We cannot do anything better for them than to trust them into his care and hardly anything worse than to try to keep them in our own.

I knew a Christian mother who trusted peacefully for her own salvation but was racked with anxiety about her sons, who seemed entirely indifferent to Christianity. One evening she heard about the possibility of putting her loved ones into the fortress of God by faith and leaving them there. Like a flash of heavenly light, she saw the inconsistency of hiding herself in God's fortress and leaving her beloved sons outside. At once her faith took them into the fortress with her, and she abandoned them to the care of God. I did not see her again for a year, but, when I did, she came up to me with a beaming face. With tears of joy filling her eyes, she said, "Rejoice with me, dear friend, that I learned how to put my boys into the fortress of God. They have been safe there ever since, and all of them are good Christians today."

23 *If God so clothes the grass of the field, which today is alive and tomorrow is thrown into the oven, will he not much more clothe you, O men of little faith?* (Mt 6:30)

To many Christians this passage, and others like it, are so familiar that they have almost lost all meaning. But they do mean something, something almost too wonderful to believe. They tell us that God cares for us human beings "much more" than he cares for the universe around us. He will watch over and provide for us much more than he will even for it.

Incredible, yet true! How often we have marveled at the orderly working of the universe, and have admired the great creative Power that made it and now controls it. But we have, none of us, I suppose, ever felt it necessary to take the burden of the universe upon our own shoulders. We have trusted the Creator to manage it all without our help.

Even where we have fully recognized that the universe is completely in God's care, we have failed to see that we are also there, and have never dreamed that it could be true that "much more" than he cares for the universe will he care for us. We have burdened ourselves with the care of ourselves. In our unbelief, we think that we are of "much less" value than the birds of the air or the lilies of the field. Man is so puny, so insignificant, of so little account, when compared to the great, wide universe. What is he, we ask, that God should care for him? Yet God declares that he does care for him and that he even cares for him much more than he cares for the universe. Much more, remember, not much less. Every thought of anxiety about ourselves must be immediately crushed with the reflection that, since we are not so foolish to become anxious about the universe, we must not be so much more foolish to become anxious about ourselves.

24 *What man of you, if his son asks him for bread, will give him a stone?* (Mt 7:9)

All human readiness to hear and answer the cry of need, can only be a faint picture of God's readiness. If parents would not give a stone for bread, neither would God. When we ask him for something, we must be absolutely sure that we will receive the "good thing" for which we asked, whether what we receive looks like it or not.

The mother of St. Augustine, in her longing for the conversion of her son, prayed that he might not go to Rome because she feared its dissipations. God answered her by sending him to Rome to be converted there. Things we call good are often evil things to God, and our evil is his good. However things may look, we always know that God must give the best, because he is God and could do no other.

25 *It is like a man going on a journey, when he leaves home and puts his servants in charge, each with his work, and commands the doorkeeper to be on the watch.*
(Mk 13:34)

"Each with his work." Not the same work to all, but each one has his own talent and his own place. And each one is responsible only for that which is given him to do. This seems too plain to be spoken of; but as a fact, most members of God's household are more concerned about the work given to someone else, than about that given to themselves.

Not what others do or leave undone, but what I myself do or leave undone, is the vital thing in my soul life. Neither should I care for the judgment of others concerning my work. A servant in a household is not anxious to know what the master or mistress next door may think of him or his work, but only what his own master and mistress think.

26 *But God, who is rich in mercy, out of the great love with which he loved us, even when we were dead through our trespasses, made us alive together with Christ (by grace you have been saved), and raised us up with him, and made us sit with him in the heavenly places in Christ Jesus. (Eph 2:4-6)*

It is just as though one had died and been buried, and had risen again, and thenceforth walked in a new and risen life. Such a one would look at things from an altogether different standpoint and measure them by other measures. Try to put yourself in the place of Lazarus after he had been raised from the dead and imagine, if you can, with what eyes he would behold the world and the things of it; and you will perhaps get a glimpse of the meaning of this resurrection life. Things once all-important to him, must have lost their value, and things once insignificant, must have become of mighty import.

The place from which we look makes all the difference in how things look. The resurrection life seats us in "heavenly places," and we look from these *down* upon earthly things, and not *up* from earthly places upon heavenly things. We are to walk through this world as those whose heart and brain move there, while our feet stay here.

27 *Well done, good and faithful servant; you have been faithful over a little, I will set you over much; enter into the joy of your master. (Mt 25:23)*

You wicked and slothful servant! . . . You ought to have invested my money with the bankers, and at my coming I should have received what was my own interest. So take the talent from him, and give it to him who has the ten talents.
(Mt 25:26-27)

In the first two cases it is "Well done, good and faithful servant," and in the last, "you wicked and slothful servant." The difference was not in the amount done or left undone, but in the faithfulness or unfaithfulness to the talents given. The servant with the two talents was commended in just the same words as the one with five. And the servant with only one talent would have received a similar approval had he shown a similar faithfulness.

For such a commendation who would not strive? To hear the Master say, "Well done" at last, would surely repay one for all that might have been passed through to deserve it!

28 *So each of us shall give account of himself to God.*
(Rom 14:12)

We cannot avoid giving this "account," for it is one that gives itself. Our life work tells in the formation of character, and it is the character we have formed that is to be the judgment given. In the very nature of things we receive according to what we have done, and we cannot help it.

"And cast the worthless servant into the outer darkness; there men will weep and gnash their teeth" (Mt 25:30). This is a very solemn word. For we see that it is the "worthless servant" merely, who was cast into this outer darkness where there is weeping and gnashing of teeth: not one who had committed some great crime, but one who had simply been unprofitable. And it was a "servant" too, not an outsider, but one of the "household." Have we ever dreamed that to be merely a "worthless servant" was so serious and grievous a thing as this?

29 *Is not this the fast that I choose: to loose the bonds of wickedness, to undo the thongs of the yoke,/to let the oppressed go free, and to break every yoke?* (Is 58:6)

All the talking, or fasting, or weeping, or wearing of sackcloth in the world, will not do as a substitute for the Christlike life of love and kindness towards our fellow human beings. The "fast that he chooses" is to help the needy and raise the fallen, and nothing will do instead of this.

A great many Christians never do anything except for

themselves. Whether they fast, or whether they eat and drink, it is all for themselves, to save their own souls, or to help forward their own experience; but they never lift a hand to help anyone else. Their religion is all for self-exaltation, in one way or another, either now or hereafter, and not truly for the glory of God at all.

30   *Truly, I say to you, this poor widow has put in more than all those who are contributing to the treasury. For they all contributed out of their abundance; but she out of her poverty has put in everything she had, her whole living.*

(Mk 12:43-44)

It is not much to give out of one's abundance; but to give "out of one's poverty," all that one has, whether in time, or in talent, or in sympathy, this is the thing that receives the Lord's approval. If then you have only one talent, and the service you render is "out of your poverty" instead of out of your abundance, even though it be all that you have, cast it into the Lord's treasury, and be sure you will win his approval, whether the world approves or not.

31   *The kingdom of heaven is like treasure hidden in a field, which a man found and covered up; then in his joy he goes and sells all that he has and buys that field. Again, the kingdom of heaven is like a merchant in search of fine pearls, who, on finding one pearl of great value, went and sold all that he had and bought it.* (Mt 13:44-46)

Christ sold "all he had" to purchase the "field," which is the world, for the sake of the "treasure" that is hidden there, which is humanity. (This is not the usual interpretation of the passage, but by comparing Christ's own words, "the field is the world," in Mt 13:38, I think we will find it admissible.)

And again, the pearl of great price may also be considered to be the human race whom Christ purchased with his own blood, with "all that he had."

Surely, after all this, we cannot question the fact of his ownership! Since, then, it is a settled fact that we are not our own, but that we belong to God, let us consider what follows from this: 1. His ownership lays upon him the responsibility of caring for us. 2. It lays upon us the responsibility of surrender, and trust, and obedience to him.

February

1 In all their affliction he was afflicted, / and the angel of his presence saved them; / in his love and in his pity he redeemed them; / he lifted them up and carried them. (Is 63:9)

When I read in the Bible that God is love, I am to believe it, just because "it is written," and not because I have had any inward revelation that it is true; and when the Bible says that he cares for us as he cares for the lilies of the field and the birds of the air, and that the very hairs of our heads are all numbered, I am to believe it, just because it is written, whether I have any inward revelation of it or not.

It is of vital importance for us to understand that the Bible is a statement, not of theories, but of actual facts. Things are not true because they are in the Bible, but they are only in the Bible because they are true.

A little boy, who had been studying at school about the discovery of America, said to his father one day, "Father, if I had been Columbus I should not have taken all that trouble to discover America." "Why, what would you have done?" asked the father. "Oh," replied the little boy, "I would just have gone to the

21

map and found it." This little boy did not understand that maps are only pictures of already-known places, and that America did not exist because it was on the map, but it could not be on the map until it was already known to exist. The Bible, like the map, is a simple statement of facts; so that when it tells us that God loves us, it is only telling us something that is a fact.

2 *Acquaint now thyself with God, and be at peace.*
(Jb 22:21, KJV)

It is not a question of acquaintance with ourselves, or of knowing what we are, or what we do, or what we feel; it is simply and only a question of becoming acquainted with God, getting to know what he is, and what he does, and what he feels. Comfort and peace can never come from anything we know about ourselves, but only and always from what we know about God. We may spend our days in what we call our religious duties and may fill our devotions with fervor, and we still may be miserable. Nothing can set our hearts at rest but a real acquaintance with God. After all, everything in our salvation must depend upon him in the last instance. If we were planning to take a dangerous voyage, our first question would be about the sort of captain we were to have. Our common sense would tell us that if the captain were untrustworthy, no amount of trustworthiness on our part would make the voyage safe; and it would be his character and not our own that would be the thing of paramount importance.

3 *Let not your hearts be troubled; believe in God, believe also in me. In my Father's house are many rooms; if it were not so, would I have told you that I go to prepare a place for you?*
(Jn 14:1-2)

We cannot have the spirit of a son, until we know we are sons. To doubt it, would be to lose the spirit at once.

Our Lord himself always speaks to his disciples in terms of absolute certainty concerning their relationship with God.

"If it were not so he would have told us." Surely we may trust him and accept his statements as facts, without any further questioning.

4 Who shall separate us from the love of Christ? Shall tribulation, or distress, or persecution, or famine, or nakedness, or peril, or sword? . . . No, in all these things we are more than conquerors through him who loved us. (Rom 8:35, 37)

No one can read the history of the words and deeds of the apostles and the early believers without seeing that they were saturated through and through with an utter certainty of their salvation in the Lord Jesus Christ. It was as much a part of them as their nationality as Jews, or their nativity in Israel, and was no more open to question. Let us try to imagine them as being filled with the doubtings and questionings of modern Christians and think what effect it would have had upon their preaching and their work. We can see in a moment that it would have been fatal to the spread of the gospel and that a church founded on doubts and questionings could have made no headway in an unbelieving world.

This tone of utter assurance runs through all the Epistles. Each is addressed to people who took for granted their standing as the reconciled and forgiven children of God; and the writers express the same assurance for themselves as they do for those to whom they write.

Again, if we run through the Epistles we shall invariably find that they also, like the Gospels and the Acts, are saturated through and through with assurance. Nowhere is a doubt or a question of the believer's standing in the family of God even so much as hinted at or supposed.

5 Then they said to him, "What must we do, to be doing the works of God?" Jesus answered them, "This is the work of God, that you believe in him whom he has sent." (Jn 6:28-29)

Every one who believes that Jesus is the Christ is a child of God, and every one who loves the parent loves the child. (1 Jn 5:1)

We must believe two things. First, what God says concerning Christ. Second, what he says concerning us.

We are not really believing a person if we only believe half of what he says; and yet many who would consider it the worst of sins to disbelieve God's testimony concerning Christ consider it no sin at all, but in fact rather virtuous humility, to doubt his testimony concerning themselves. They dare not doubt that Jesus is the Christ but find no difficulty in doubting whether they themselves are children of God. Yet God joins the two inseparably together. Here is a plain and simple statement. "Everyone who believes, *is* a child of God"; not will be, but is, now in the present moment; for no one can believe who is not born a child of God.

6 *You shall know that I, the Lord, am your Savior / and your Redeemer, the Mighty one of Jacob. (Is 60:16)*

On that day you will know that I am in my Father, and you in me, and I in you. (Jn 14:20)

This assurance of who God is and who we are *in him* is necessary for all right living. It ought to be the first step in the Christian life. In the absence of this assurance lies the secret of much of the failure of Christians. They present the strange anomaly of children who doubt their parentage, of heirs who are afraid to take possession of their inheritance, of a bride who is not sure she is really married.

What could we expect from such doubts in earthly relationships but indifference, fear, anxiety, unkindness, sorrow, and rebellion? Are not these the very things that are found far too often in the hearts of God's children, in reference to their relationship with him?

7 *Let us draw near with a true heart in full assurance of faith, with our hearts sprinkled clean from an evil conscience and our bodies washed with pure water. (Heb 10:22)*

By the assurance of faith is meant a clear and definite knowledge of the forgiveness of sins, of reconciliation with God, and of our relationship with him as our Father. About these vital matters we must be able to say, "I know." Not "I hope so," or "I wish so," but firmly and unhesitatingly, "I know."

No soul can serve the Lord with joyfulness who is in doubt about the reality or the stability of its relationship with him. All human comfort is destroyed when such doubt affects earthly relationships; and little divine comfort is to be found in doubts about our spiritual relationships.

Can we then suppose for a moment that this too frequent reign of doubt in Christians' hearts was God's plan for his people? Does the Bible teach that it is? I answer most emphatically, no, a thousand times no!

8 *"I am the Alpha and the Omega," says the Lord God, who is and who was and who is to come, the Almighty.* (Rv 1:8)

These simple words "I am," express eternity and the unchangeableness of existence, which is the very first element necessary in a God who is to be depended upon. None of us could depend on a changeable God. He must be the same yesterday, today, and forever, if we are to have any peace or comfort.

But is this all his name implies, simply "I am"? I am, what?—we ask. What does this "I am" include? I believe it includes everything the human heart longs for and needs. This unfinished name of God seems to me like a blank check signed by a rich friend, given to us to be filled up with whatever sum we may desire. The whole Bible tells us what it means.

Every attribute of God, every revelation of his character, every proof of his undying love, every declaration of his watchful care, every assertion of his purposes of tender mercy, every manifestation of his loving kindness, all are the filling out of this unfinished "I am."

God tells us through all the pages of his book what he is. "I am," he says, all that my people need: "I am" their strength; "I am" their wisdom; "I am" their righteousness; "I am" their peace; "I am" their salvation; "I am" their life; "I am" their all in all.

9 *No one has ever seen God; the only Son, who is in the bosom of the Father, he has made him known.* (Jn 1:18)

Christ, then, is the revelation of God. None of us have seen God, and we never can see him in this present stage of our existence, for we have not the faculties that would make it possible. But he has incarnated himself in Christ, and we can see Christ, since he was a man like one of us.

A man who wants to talk with ants might stand over an ant hill and harangue for a whole day and not one word would reach the ears of the ants. They would run to and fro, utterly unconscious of his presence. As far as we know, ants have no faculties by which they can receive human communications. But if a man could incarnate himself in the body of an ant, and could go among them, living an ant's life and speaking their language, he could make himself intelligible to them at once. Incarnation is always necessary when a higher form of life would communicate with a lower.

Christ revealed God by what he was, by what he did, and by what he said. From the cradle to the grave, every moment of his life was a revelation of God. We must go to him then for our knowledge of God, and we must refuse to believe anything concerning God that is not revealed to us in Christ. All other revelations are partial and therefore not wholly true. Only in Christ do we see God as he is; for Christ is declared to be the "express image" of God.

10 *The fear of the Lord is the beginning of wisdom.*
(Ps 111:10)

The fear that the psalmist refers to is fear that stems from love, not from fright. It is the fear of grieving or wounding the heart of a loved one; it is not the fear of consequences to ourselves but rather of inflicting sorrow on someone else. It is a fear which can exist only in connection with the highest and tenderest forms of love, for all lower forms of affection are indifferent to it and cannot even comprehend it. Therefore, I believe that it is only the one who has passed through the death to self described in Job, and has learned the life of trust so evident in the Psalms, who can understand this sweet and constraining "fear of the Lord." Others may perhaps be *afraid* of him, but only these can *fear* him. Others may dread his anger, but only these alone can fear his grief. Only these know that he can be grieved, for they alone know how he loves. It is because his love for us is so deep and so tender that we are able to grieve him, for no other affection or passion of the soul can be grieved but love. None can truly fear him, therefore, who do not know something of his love, and none can, I believe, truly follow him who do not know this sweet constraining fear. For his voice is so gentle and low, and his will comes to us so much more often in the form of suggestion rather than in that of command, that unless our love makes us fear the slightest neglect of his sweet requirements, or the least deviation from his will, we shall often overlook them and miss them altogether. No wonder that we are told here that the "fear of the Lord is the beginning of wisdom." For he alone is wise who follows the Lord wherever he leads, and such a following is the outcome only of this lovely fear.

11

Truly, truly, I say to you, we speak of what we know, and bear witness to what we have seen. (Jn 3:11)

When Nicodemus came to Jesus by night to ask him how the things he was saying could possibly be true, Jesus told him that they were still true, regardless of whether he understood them or not. No one who believes in Christ at all, can doubt that he knew God; and no one can question whether or not we ought to receive his testimony. Jesus has assured us over and over that he knew what he was talking about and that what he said was to be received as the absolute truth, because he had come down from heaven and therefore knew about heavenly things.

None of us would dare openly to question the truth of this; and yet a great many of God's children utterly ignore Christ's testimony and choose instead to listen to the testimony of their own doubting hearts, which tells them it is impossible that God could be as loving in his care for us, or as tender towards our weakness and foolishness, or as ready to forgive our sins, as Christ has revealed him to be. Yet Jesus declares of himself over and over that he was a living manifestation of the Father. In all he said and did he assures us that he was simply saying and doing that which the Father would have said and done had he acted directly out of heaven from his heavenly throne.

In the face of such unqualified assertions as these, out of the lips of our Lord himself, it becomes, not only our privilege, but our duty to cast out of our conception of God every element that disagrees with the revelation made by Jesus Christ.

12   *As one whom his mother comforts, so I will comfort you.* (Is 66:13)

Notice the "*as*" and "*so*" in this passage; "*as* one whom his mother comforts *so* I will comfort you." It is real comfort that is meant here, the sort of comfort that the child feels when it is dandled on its mother's knees and carried in her arms. And yet how many of us have really believed that God's comforting is actually as tender and true as a mother's comforting, or even half or a quarter as real? Instead of thinking of ourselves as being "dandled" on his knees and hugged to his heart, have we not rather been inclined to look upon God as a stern, unbending judge, holding us at a distance, demanding our respectful homage, critical of our slightest faults? Is it any wonder that our religion, instead of making us comfortable, has made us thoroughly uncomfortable? Who could help being uncomfortable in the presence of such a judge?

But I rejoice to say that that stern judge is not there. He does not exist. The God who does exist is a God who is like a mother, a God who says to us as plainly as words can say it, "*as* one whom his mother comforts, *so* I will comfort you."

13   *This is my comfort in my affliction / that thy promise gives me life.* (Ps 119:50)

You may ask whether the Divine Comforter does not sometimes reprove us for our sins and whether we can get any comfort out of this. In my opinion this is exactly one of the places where the comfort comes in. For what sort of creatures should we be, if we had no Divine Teacher always at hand to show us our faults and awaken in us a desire to get rid of them?

If I am walking along the street with a very disfiguring hole in the back of my dress of which I am in ignorance, it is certainly a very great comfort to me to have a kind friend who will tell me of it. Similarly, it is indeed a comfort to know that there is always abiding with me a divine, all-seeing Comforter, who will reprove me for all my faults and will not let me go on in a fatal unconsciousness of them. Emerson says it is far more to a man's interest that he should see his own faults, than that any one else should see them. A moment's thought will convince us that this is true and will make us thankful for the Comforter who reveals them to us.

14 *Therefore, behold, I will allure her, / and bring her into the wilderness, and speak tenderly to her. (Hos 2:14)*

We find ourselves in a "wilderness" of disappointment and of suffering, and we wonder why the God who loves us should have allowed it. But he knows that it is only in that very wilderness that we can hear and receive the tender words he has to pour out upon us. We must feel the *need* of comfort before we can listen to the *words* of comfort. And God knows that it is infinitely better and happier for us to need his comforts and receive them than to be without them. The consolations of God mean the substituting of a far higher and better thing than the things we lose to get them. The things we lose are earthly things; those God substitutes are heavenly. Paul said he counted all things as loss if he might but win Christ; and, if we have even the faintest glimpse of what winning Christ means, we will say so too.

15 *Blessed are those who mourn, for they shall be comforted. (Mt 5:4)*

While it is easy for us to accept the truth of this word when we are happy and do not need comforting, we find it almost impossible to believe the moment tragedy or difficulty strikes. Unconsciously, we reverse the words of the Bible so that they say, "Blessed are they that rejoice, for they, and they only, shall be comforted." It is very strange how often in our secret hearts we alter the word a little, making the meaning exactly opposite of the original; or else we put in so many "ifs" and "buts" that we take the whole point out of what is said. Consider, for instance, those beautiful words, "God who comforts those that are cast down" and ask yourselves whether you have never been tempted to make it read, "God who forsakes those who are cast down," or, "God who overlooks those who are cast down"; or "God who will comfort those who are cast down if they show themselves worthy of comfort"; and whether, consequently, instead of being comforted, you have not been plunged into misery and despair.

The psalmist tells us that God will "comfort us on every side," and what an all-embracing bit of comfort this is—*on every side*. Yet, in times of special trial, how many Christians secretly read this as though it said, "God will comfort us on every side except just the side where our trials lie." But God says every side, and it is only unbelief that leads us to make an exception.

16 *Can a woman forget her sucking child, / that she should have no compassion on the son of her womb? / Even these may forget, yet I will not forget you. (Is 49:15)*

You may ask how you are to get hold of divine comfort. My answer is that you must take it. God's comfort is being continually and abundantly given, but unless you will accept it, you cannot have it. Unless you will believe that he has not forgotten you, you will act as though he has.

Divine comfort does not come to us in any mysterious or arbitrary way. It comes as the result of a divine method. The indwelling Comforter reminds us of comforting things concerning our Lord, and, if we believe them, we are comforted by them. A text is brought to our mind, or the verse of a hymn, or some thought concerning the love of Christ and his tender care for us. If we receive the suggestion in simple faith, we cannot help being comforted. But if we refuse to listen to the voice of our Comforter and insist instead on listening to the voice of discouragement or despair, no comfort can by any possibility reach our souls.

17 *For the Lord God helps me; therefore I have not been confounded; / therefore I have set my face like a flint, / and I know that I shall not be put to shame.* (Is 50:7)

We must make up our minds to believe every single word of comfort God has ever spoken; and we must refuse utterly to listen to any words of discomfort spoken by our own hearts or by our circumstances. We must set our faces like a flint to believe in the Divine Comforter under each and every sorrow and trial, and to accept and rejoice in his all-embracing comfort. I say, "set our faces like a flint," because, when everything around us seems out of sorts, it is not always easy to believe God's words of comfort. We must put our will into this matter of being comforted, just as we have to put our will into all other matters in our spiritual life. We must choose to be comforted.

18 *Though the fig tree do not blossom, / nor fruit be on the vines. . . . yet I will rejoice in the Lord, / I will joy in the God of my salvation.* (Hb 3:17-18)

We are made to find our joy in the Lord, and we cannot find rest short of it. All God's dealings with us, therefore, are shaped to this end; and he is often obliged to deprive us of all joy in everything else, in order to force us to find our joy only in him. It is all very well, perhaps, to rejoice in his promises, or to rejoice in the revelations he may have granted us, or in the experiences we may have realized. But to rejoice in the Promiser himself—without promises, experiences, or revelations—this is the crowning point of Christian life; and this is the only place where we can know the peace which passes all understanding and which nothing can disturb.

19 *The Lord is my shepherd, I shall not want.* (Ps 23:1)

You may have repeated these words hundreds of times. But have you ever really believed it to be an actual fact? Have you felt safe and happy and free from care, as a sheep must feel when under the care of a good shepherd? Or have you felt yourself to be like a poor forlorn sheep without a shepherd, or with an unfaithful, inefficient shepherd, who does not supply your needs, and who leaves you in times of danger and darkness?

I beg of you to answer this question honestly in your own souls. If you feel more like the forlorn sheep, how can you reconcile your condition with the statement the Lord is your Shepherd, and therefore you shall not want? You say, he is your Shepherd, and yet you complain that you do want. Who has made the mistake? You or the Lord?

But here, perhaps, you will meet me with the words, "Oh, no, I do not blame the Lord, but I am so weak and foolish and ignorant, that I am not worthy of his care." But do you not know that sheep are always weak, and helpless, and silly; and that the very reason they are compelled to have a shepherd to care for them is just because they are so unable to take care of themselves? Their welfare and their safety, therefore, do not in the least depend upon their own strength, nor upon their own wisdom, nor upon anything in themselves, but wholly and entirely upon the care of their shepherd. If you are a sheep, your welfare must depend altogether upon your Shepherd and not at all upon yourself.

20 *I saw all Israel scattered upon the mountains, as sheep that have no shepherd.* (1 Kgs 22:17)

We all understand the reponsibility of the shepherd in the case of sheep; but the moment we transfer the figure to our religion, we at once shift all the responsibility from the Shepherd's shoulders and lay it upon the sheep. We demand of the poor human sheep the wisdom, and care, and power to provide, that can only belong to the Divine Shepherd and be met by him; and of course the poor human sheep fail.

I freely confess there is a difference between sheep and ourselves: they have neither the intelligence nor the power to withdraw themselves from the care of their shepherd, while we have. Silly as sheep are, we well know that no sheep could be so silly that it refuses the care of the shepherd. We are so much wiser than sheep, in our own estimation, that we think the sort of trust that sheep exercise will not do for us; and, in our superior intelligence, we presume to take matters into our own hands, and so shut ourselves out from the Shepherd's care.

I entreat you to face this matter honestly. For not only your own welfare and comfort are dependent upon your right apprehension of this blessed relation, but also the glory of your Shepherd is at stake. Have you ever thought of the grief and dishonor this sad condition of yours brings upon him? The credit of a shepherd depends upon the condition of his flock. Now, the Lord makes statements about himself as a Good Shepherd. He is telling the universe, the world, and the church, "I am the Good Shepherd"; and if they ask, "Where are the sheep? What condition are they in?" can he point to us as being a credit to his care? The universe is looking on to see what the Lord Jesus Christ is able to make of us and what kind of sheep we are, whether we are well fed, and healthy, and happy. Their verdict concerning him will largely depend upon what they see in us.

21 *But let him ask in faith, with no doubting, for he who doubts is like a wave of the sea that is driven and tossed by the wind. For that person must not suppose that a double-minded man, unstable in all his ways, will receive anything from the Lord. (Jas 1:6-8)*

It is of no use to fight against this inevitable law. As well might the architect try to work in opposition to the law of gravitation and undertake to build his house from the top downwards, as for the Christian to try to accomplish anything in the spiritual realm by means of doubt. It simply cannot be done; and the sooner Christians know this the better for them.

How much can be done by faith may remain an open question, perhaps, but it is a settled matter that nothing can be done by doubt.

Faith is, I believe, the vital principle of the spiritual life, just as truly as breath seems to be the vital principle of the bodily life; and we can no more live spiritually without faith than we can live our bodily life without breath.

22 *Those who belong to Christ Jesus have crucified the flesh with its passions and desires.* (Gal 5:24)

To crucify, means *to put to death,* not to keep alive in misery. But so obscured has the whole subject become to the children of God, that I believe a great many feel as if they were crucifying self when they are simply seating self on a pinnacle and are tormenting it and making it miserable. We will undergo the most painful self-sacrifices, and call it "taking up the cross," and will find great satisfaction in it; and all the time we will fail to understand that the true cross consists in counting the flesh, or the "old man," as an utterly worthless thing, fit only to be put to death. There is a subtle enjoyment in torturing the outward self, if only the interior self-life may be fed thereby. A man will make himself a fakir, if it is only self that does it, so that self can share in the glory. The flesh of man likes to have some credit; it cannot bear to be counted as dead and therefore ignored; and in all religions of legality it has a chance. This explains, I am sure, why there is so much legality among Christians. But did we read the scriptures correctly, we should see that the carnal mind, i.e., the fleshly mind (as it is literally translated), cannot serve God nor enter into his kingdom, no matter how much we may try by all sorts of asceticism to make it fit.

23 *But far be it from me to glory except in the cross of our Lord Jesus Christ, by which the world has been crucified to me, and I to the world.* (Gal 6:14)

By being crucified to the world, Paul meant that he was dead to it. He did not mean that he was still alive to it and was being made to suffer because he must give it up. He was absolutely dead to it, so that it no longer had any attractions for him. To be dead to a thing must mean that the thing has no power to attract. This is precisely what is meant in the Bible by "taking up the cross." It is to become so dead to the world (that is, the lower plane of living) that its power to tempt is gone. It is to have our affections so set on things above, that merely earthly things have lost their charm.

24 *Each one must do as he has made up his mind, not reluctantly or under compulsion, for God loves a cheerful giver.* (2 Cor 9:7)

To my mind, grudging service is no more acceptable to God than it would be to us; and such an idea of the "cross" as this, seems to me a very poor and low substitute for the glorious truth of our death with Christ and our resurrection into the triumphant spiritual life hid with Christ in God. Surely, if we are born of God, we must love the things God loves and hate the things he hates; and if we are one with Christ, it is out of the question that we should chafe against his will or find his service hard! Is it a sign of the highest sort of union between a husband and wife when the one finds it a great trial to please the other? Ought it not rather to be a joy to do so? How much more is this true as regards our relations with Christ?

25 *No one born of God commits sin; for God's nature abides in him, and he cannot sin because he is born of God.* (1 Jn 3:9)

That part of us which is born of God, the spiritual man in us, cannot sin, because it is holy in its very nature or essence. If we sin, therefore, it must be because we have permitted that in us which is born of the flesh to have some life and have submitted ourselves, i.e., our personality, more or less to its control. Not only would I say this concerning sin, but I would also say it concerning that shrinking from and dislike of God's will which so many Christians think constitutes the cross. The spiritual man in us cannot dislike God's will, for in the very nature of things that which is born of God must love the will of God. That which shrinks therefore and suffers, must be the self-life; and the self-life we are commanded to crucify and deny (Mk 8:34-35).

To deny anything means that you do not recognize its existence. To deny ourselves, therefore, does not mean to keep self alive and let it be made miserable by forcing it to do God's will; but it means to deny the very existence of self and to live only in that part of our nature that loves God's will and delights to do it.

26 *It cannot be gotten for gold, / and silver cannot be weighed as its price. . . . the price of wisdom is above pearls.* (Jb 28:15, 18)

The relation of knowledge to wisdom is extremely important. Knowledge is the indispensable foundation of reason and judgment, and without the necessary ideas, wise conclusions cannot be formed. A man is often unable to determine what is right without the aid of knowledge, and an ignorant person cannot act wisely except by instinct or accident. Knowledge may exist without wisdom, but wisdom cannot exist without knowledge. The minds of many persons are filled with knowledge of very little value, and it is well known that extensive knowledge, and even a university education, may, and often do, coexist with untruthfulness, dishonesty, and so on. But wisdom and immorality cannot coexist in the same person.

"Wisdom," according to Lamarck, "consists in the observation of a certain number of rules or virtues—viz., love of truth in all things; the need of improving one's mind; moderation in desires; decorum in all actions; a wise reserve in unessential wants; indulgence, toleration, humanity, goodwill towards all men; love of the public good; contempt for weakness; a kind of severity towards oneself which preserves us from that multitude of artificial wants enslaving those who give up to them; resignation and, if possible, moral impassibility in suffering reverses, injustices, oppression, and losses; respect for order, for public institutions, civil authorities, laws, and morality."

27 *As a father pities his children, / so the Lord pities those who fear him. / For he knows our frame; / he remembers that we are dust.* (Ps 103:13-14)

But you say, "What about the other names of God, do they not convey other and more terrifying ideas?" They only do so because this blessed name of Father is not added to them. This name must underlie every other name by which he has ever been known. Has he been called a Judge? Yes, but he is a Father Judge, one who judges as a loving father would. Is he a King? Yes, but he is a King who is at the same time the Father of his subjects, and who rules them with a father's tenderness. Is he a Lawgiver? Yes, but he is a Lawgiver who gives laws as a father would, remembering the weakness and ignorance of his helpless children.

Never, never must we think of God in any other way than as "our Father." All other attributes with which we endow him in our conception must be based upon and limited by this one. What a good father could not do, God, who is our Father, cannot do either, and what a good father ought to do, God, who is our Father, is absolutely sure to do.

28 *Fear not, little flock, for it is your Father's good pleasure to give you the kingdom.* (Lk 12:32)

It is not only that our Heavenly Father is willing to give us good things. He is far more than willing. There is no grudging in his giving; it is his "good pleasure" to give; he likes to do it. He wants to give you the kingdom far more than you want to have it. Why then should we ask him for things in such fear and trembling, and why should we torment ourselves with anxiety lest he should fail to grant what we need?

We are told that we are of the "household of God." The

principle is announced in the Bible, that if any man fails to provide for his own household, he has "denied the faith and is worse than an infidel." Since then we are of the "household of God," this principle applies to him, and if he should fail to provide for us, his own words would condemn him. I say this reverently, but I want to say it emphatically, for so few people seem to have realized it.

29 *Cast all your anxieties on him, for he cares about you.*
(1 Pt 5:7)

If God is our Father, the only thing we can do with doubts, and fears, and anxious thoughts, is to cast them all behind our backs forever and have nothing more to do with them. We *can* do this. We can give up our doubts just as we would urge a drunkard to give up his drink. We can take a pledge against doubting, just as we try to induce the drunkard to take a pledge against drinking. If once we realize that our doubts are an actual sin against God and imply a question of his trustworthiness, we will be eager to renounce them. We may have cherished our doubts heretofore because we have thought they were a becoming attitude of soul in one so unworthy; but if we now see that God is in truth our Father, we will reject every doubt with horror, as being a libel on our Father's love and our Father's care.

March

1   Then the word of the Lord came to me: "O house of Israel, can I not do with you as this potter has done? says the Lord. Behold, like the clay in the potter's hand, so are you in my hand, O house of Israel." (Jer 18:5-6)

It takes us a great while to learn that God is really our Maker and not we ourselves; and a large part of the perplexities of our spiritual experience arise from this ignorance. We are continually taking ourselves out of the hands of our Divine Maker by our efforts to make, or remake, or unmake ourselves. The Potter desires to fashion us into a beautiful vessel for his honor, but we will not hold still and let him work. We interfere with his processes, either by resisting him, or by trying to help him, and so the vessel is marred in his hands.

If we realize that we are God's workmanship and not our own, we will lie still in his hands and will abandon ourselves to his working.

2   Then God said, "Let us make man in our image, after our likeness; and let them have dominion over the fish of the sea, and over the birds of the air." (Gn 1:26)

Of course this did not mean a likeness of person or body, but likeness of character and nature; that is, we are "to be perfect as he is perfect," in the same sort of perfection, not as to degree of course, but as to quality. We cannot see God to know what we are to be like; but we see him incarnated in Christ, who is declared to be the "express image" of God; and thus we can look upon and consider the image to which we are to be conformed.

We can never understand a complicated machine until we know its maker's purpose regarding it. How did he mean it to work? What was it intended to accomplish? How has he arranged for it to run? When we walk through an exhibition of machinery we ask continually, as we stop to look at one machine after another, "What is this for?" "What is that for?" We are sure, when we see a machine, that the maker intended it to accomplish some special end; and we cannot imagine any man being so stupid as to make a machine that is not meant to accomplish anything.

Our Divine Maker, therefore, has made us for a purpose, and we must seek to understand that purpose.

3 *You shall receive power when the Holy Spirit has come upon you; and you shall be my witnesses in Jerusalem and in all Judea and Samaria and to the end of the earth.* (Acts 1:8)

Every machine of man's making is intended to operate by some definite sort of power: manpower, water power, or some other method. In every case the machine is made for its own power and will not operate for any other.

We are made to go by Holy Spirit power, and we cannot go right without it.

If we try to work ourselves by our own power we shall utterly fail, for we have no natural powers that can control spiritual forces. Only the powers that belong to the spiritual nature can have dominion over these.

4 *Whither shall I go from thy Spirit? / Or whither shall I flee from thy presence? / If I ascend to heaven, thou art there! / If I make my bed in Sheol, thou art there!* (Ps 139:7-8)

The all-pervading presence of God with us is the one absolutely certain and unchangeable thing amid all that is so doubtful and changeable in this world of ours. Yet very few people realize this. Even Christians will cry out for the Lord to "come" to them, as though he had gone off on a journey or were in the remote realms of space. "How can I get into his presence?" they ask with eager longing; when all the while they are already in his presence and cannot by any possibility get out of it, not even if they "make their bed in hell," or if they live in the furthest part of the earth. Even there, wherever it may be, shall his hand hold and lead them.

5 *If I say, "Let only darkness cover me, and the light about me be night," / even the darkness is not dark to thee, the night is bright as the day; / for darkness is as light with thee.*

(Ps 139:11-12)

"Even the darkness is not dark to thee." We all know this must be a fact, in the very nature of things; and yet when the soul finds itself in spiritual darkness, it seems impossible to believe that it can be true. The fever of delirium may hide the mother from the child, and her heart may be wrung by its piteous cries for her coming, but the child's blindness does not drive away the mother nor make her ears deaf to its cries. And just so the delirium of our doubts or despair or even of our sins, while it hides him from us so that we call out in anguish for his presence, can never hide us from him, for the "darkness is as light" to him.

If our faith will but grasp this fact as a reality, our "seasons of darkness" will not trouble us, for we shall be sure all the while, although we cannot see him nor feel him, that he is still there close at hand for our need, an "ever-present" help in all our trouble.

6 *I am continually with thee; / thou dost hold my right hand. . . . / Whom have I in heaven but thee! / And there is nothing upon earth that I desire besides thee. / My flesh and my heart may fail, / but God is the strength of my heart and my portion for ever.* (Ps 73:23-25)

"My flesh and my heart may fail," but the ever-present God still holds us by our right hand, even though we may not realize it; he is our all-sufficient portion for ever.

But some may ask whether there is not such a thing as "coming into" his presence and "leaving" it, being nearer or further off from him. To this I answer that these are only figures of speech which express spiritual states on our part and not any divine facts on God's part. I may be seated close to a person and yet be separated in spirit from that person by thousands of miles. When we speak of nearness or distance regarding God, it is only according to our spirits, not according to the facts. He is always near us, but we are not always near him. In fact, he is so close to us that it isn't even accurate to speak of him as being near. He created us, and if we only knew the facts of the case, it would be as impossible for us to think of ourselves apart from him, as to think of ourselves apart from ourselves.

I feel sure our modes of speech in regard to this subject have led us into great darkness. We pray, "O Lord, come to us," when we ought to pray, "O Lord, make us come!" The "coming" is altogether in our spirits, not in his presence.

7 *When he came to himself he said, "How many of my father's hired servants have bread enough and to spare, but I perish here with hunger! I will arise and go to my father, and I will say to him, 'Father, I have sinned against heaven and before you; I am no longer worthy to be called your son; treat me as one of your hired servants.'"* (Lk 15:17-19)

In all living there is one principal center around which life revolves and for the sake of which it acts. Generally this center is the "I" or self. Everything is calculated with reference to its influence on self; what gain or what improvement to one's personal standing or prospects will come from certain courses of action? How will it affect *me?* These are the continual underlying questions. The prodigal son is an illustration of this.

The son had no thought of the father's love or sorrow or longing; his only care was to get comfort and food for himself;

and his expectations could rise no higher than to be a servant in his father's household, where he would find "food to spare."

This is always the first selfish way of the human heart; we do not consider how our heavenly Father loves us, and longs for us, and grieves over our wandering, and will rejoice at our return; but we ask what *we* shall get by returning, what personal gain will accrue to *us*, how much better off *we* shall be for giving our allegiance to Christ. It is the "I" religion only, that we can comprehend at first.

8 But the father said to his servants, "Bring quickly the best robe, and put it on him; and put a ring on his hand, and shoes on his feet; and bring the fatted calf and kill it, and let us eat and make merry; for this my son was dead, and is alive again; he was lost, and is found." (Lk 15:22-24)

Thus, the prodigal son is welcomed home. He came home because he was starving and because he realized that his father's servants had plenty to eat. He would ask his father to forgive him and to treat him like a hired servant.

In the father's embrace the "I" religion is swept away, and all thoughts of being a "hired man, with food to spare" vanish before the "best robe," and the "fatted calf," and the merry feast of welcome over "the son who was dead and is alive."

Sooner or later the child of God, if his spiritual life develops as it ought, comes to this place of insight, where thoughts of self vanish in the wondrous revelation of the Father's heart.

9 He who is a hireling and not a shepherd, whose own the sheep are not, sees the wolf coming and leaves the sheep and flees; and the wolf snatches them and scatters them....I am the good shepherd;...I lay down my life for the sheep.

(Jn 10:12, 14-15)

It is impossible to imagine a good shepherd forgetting or forsaking his sheep. In fact, it is his duty to stick by them under all circumstances and to watch over them and care for them every moment. And the God who is thus revealed to us as the Good Shepherd must necessarily be as faithful to his responsibilities as an earthly shepherd is required to be to his. His care of us may be a hidden care, but it is none the less real, and all things in the daily events of our lives are made to serve his gracious purposes towards us. He may seem to have forgotten us or to have neglected us, but it can never be anything but appearances, for it would be impossible for the God who is revealed to us in the face of Jesus Christ to do such a thing.

10 *If any man would come after me, let him deny himself and take up his cross daily and follow me. For whoever would save his life will lose it; and whoever loses his life for my sake, he will save it.* (Lk 9:23-24)

The "not I" religion is the religion that denies self, that says to this "I," "I am a stranger to you and do not wish to have anything to do with you." It denies self, not in the sense of making self miserable, or of setting self on a pinnacle and sticking prongs into it to hurt it; but in the sense of utterly refusing to recognize its claims or even its existence, and of enthroning the Christ-life in its place always and everywhere.

To "take up the cross" does not mean to make this "I" miserable, as is too often thought. It means to put this "I" to death, to crucify it; not to make it suffer but to kill it outright. It means to lose our own self-life truly and literally and to have the divine life, the life hid with Christ in God, to reign in its stead.

11 *You sit and speak against your brother; / you slander your own mother's son. / These things you have done and I have been silent; / you thought that I was one like yourself. / But now I rebuke you, and lay the charge before you.*
(Ps 50:20-21)

Even Christians speak continually, not of God's great goodness, but of their brother's great failures and try to exalt themselves at their brother's expense. Naturally, they transfer the same selfish characteristics to God and think he also is entirely absorbed in the advancement of his own glory, no matter at whose expense.

But true Christianity does just the opposite. It has handed self over bodily to death and has ceased to be interested in it. It has forgotten self in its absorption in God. It expects nothing from self but everything from God; and it demands nothing for self, but seeks to lavish all on the Lord.

12 *I have been crucified with Christ; it is no longer I who live, but Christ who lives in me; and the life I now live in the flesh I live by faith in the Son of God, who loved me and gave himself for me.* (Gal 2:20)

Not only were we made alive in the first place by Christ, but moment by moment we must live in him. When temptations arise, we must no longer try to conquer them ourselves; we must not meet them with our own resolves or our own efforts; we must meet them simply with the Lord. We must hide in him as within the walls of a Gibraltar and make him our "strong refuge." In the language of one writer, we must say to him, "Lord, thou hast declared that sin shall not have dominion over thy people. I believe this word of thine cannot be broken; and therefore, helpless in myself, I rely upon thy faithfulness to save me from the dominion of the sins which now tempt me. Put forth thy power, O Lord Christ, and get thyself great glory in subduing my flesh, with its affections and lusts." Having thus committed our temptations to him, we must believe that he has decided to deliver us, and we must leave ourselves in his care. We must stand by and let him fight. We shall find, to our unutterable rejoicing, that he *does* deliver according to his word. The enemy flees from his presence, and the soul is enabled to be "more than conqueror" through him.

13 *Because you have eaten of the tree / of which I commanded you, / "You shall not eat of it," / cursed is the ground because of you; / in toil you shall eat of it all the days of your life; / thorns and thistles it shall bring forth to you.*
(Gn 3:17-18)

The story of man as developed in Genesis is one of repeated and most grievous failure. It has always seemed to me to be a vivid picture of the experience of the awakened soul, seeking to make itself what it ought to be by continually repeated efforts of its own, and ending at last by finding itself in apparently hopeless Egyptian bondage.

All of us, doubtless, know something of this experimentally. We know what it is to have set ourselves to the work of our own reformation, to have been continually turning over a "new leaf" on our birthdays, or at the start of a new year, thinking always that each renewed effort would surely be successful, and laying the blame for every failure on some fault in our circumstances or surroundings. And we remember well, some of us at least, the final and hopeless disappointment when we discovered, beyond a shadow of a doubt, that we were utterly helpless, and then the joy that came, when in our helplessness we threw ourselves upon the mercy of God and found in Christ the redemption our souls had so long sought for in vain.

14 *None is righteous, no, not one; / no one understands, no one seeks God. / All have turned aside, together they have gone wrong; / no one does good, not even one.*

(Rom 3:10-12)

In Romans 1, 2, and 3:1-20, man's hopeless and undone condition by nature is declared to us, summed up with a description of our bondage. This bondage must be acknowledged before redemption can be declared. It is only the sinner that stands in the Savior's path. It is the lost sheep that the Shepherd goes out to seek. It is in our weakness alone that his strength can be made perfect.

Have you learned this lesson? Or are you still seeking to effect your own redemption by your efforts and resolutions and fondly hoping to turn over at last the final new leaf which shall contain nothing but a record of righteousness? Are you in short trying to save yourselves, or are you letting Christ save you? Only your own hearts can answer these questions, and I pray for your souls' sakes that they may be honestly and speedily answered.

15 Moses said to the people, "Fear not, stand firm, and see the salvation of the Lord, which he will work for you today; for the Egyptians whom you see today, you shall never see again. The Lord will fight for you, and you have only to be still."
(Ex 14:13-14)

Human beings want to do something to deliver themselves, but God puts us where we cannot do anything and then says, "be still" and see what I will do. To stand still and see means simply to believe in God's record of what he has done. I "see" an event in history which I believe on the authority of another, with greater understanding than if I had been actually present at the time. Thus by faith we may "see" the path made for us out of our bondage, as plainly as the Israelites saw the one made for them. God tells us, as he told them, to leave the house of bondage and go forward. "Take the deliverance I have provided." Or in other words, "I have put away your sins by the sacrifice of myself. You do not need to ask me to do it, for it is done. Believe it, and reckon yourselves to be free."

16 Miriam and Aaron spoke against Moses . . . and they said, "Has the Lord indeed spoken only through Moses? Has he not spoken through us also?" (Nm 12:1-2)

The soul filled with the love of Christ has lost the spirit of judging. The divine charity poured into the heart "thinks no evil." But an inward lack of union with Christ always leads the soul to climb up on the judgment seat and to take upon itself the task of removing the speck out of its brother's eye, regardless of the beam in its own. God deals with all such, however, sooner or later, and sounds in the inmost ear the solemn question, "Why then were you not afraid to speak against my servant Moses?" (12:8). And in mercy he reproves and chastens until the sin is acknowledged and the soul restored.

17   *Caleb quieted the people before Moses, and said, "Let us go up at once, and occupy it; for we are well able to overcome it." Then the men who had gone up with him said, "We are not able to go up against the people; for they are stronger than we." (Nm 13:30-31)*

The Israelites refused to believe that God could deliver the promised land into their hands. They were overwhelmed by the giants they saw dwelling there. This whole scene is a picture, I think, of a stage of Christian experience, which is only too common. The soul, which has been transferred out of the kingdom of darkness into the kingdom of God's dear Son, is brought face to face with the wonderful promises and blessings of the gospel and longs to go up and possess them. The glorious liberty and triumphs, for instance, of the eighth chapter of Romans confront us, and we ask, "Is it not our privilege to enter into these things now?" But we are met on every hand by "spies," who tell us of the giants in our way and of the difficulties that we shall not be able to overcome; and thus we become so discouraged that we finally give up in despair, as Israel did, afraid to take possession of the very land of promise which the Lord our God declares he has given us, and into which it was the very purpose of our redemption that we should be brought.

18   *Behold, I will rain bread from heaven for you; and the people shall go out and gather a day's portion every day. (Ex 16:4)*

The feeding with manna described in Exodus 16 is typical of the soul of the believer feeding on Christ, as is plainly shown us in John 6:31-35. Our food is Christ, and Christ only. Not our frames, nor feelings, nor experiences, but Christ. And to feed on him, and not on them, requires that we should turn away from them wholly and not dwell on them, examine them, or even think about them, but that we should think always and only of him and see nothing but his work and his love.

19 *The Lord said to Moses, "Come up to me on the mountain, and wait there; and I will give you the tables of stone, with the law and the commandment, which I have written for their instruction." (Ex 24:12)*

The giving of the law comes in chapters 19 to 24 of Exodus, after the people were brought out of Egypt. The place this occupies, following and not preceding redemption, seems very significant to me. Man's thought always is, obedience first and redemption afterwards, but God's way is, first redemption and then obedience. First the tree, then its fruits. Obedience is in fact only possible where redemption has taken place. Israel in Egypt could not have kept God's law. The first event in any life must always be the birth into that life. The child obeys the father's laws only after he is born into that father's family. The slave can begin a life of liberty only after he has been set free. To demand from either child or slave the fruits and development of their lives before the life itself is given would be folly indeed. Let us never then say to ourselves or to one another, "You cannot be redeemed until you obey"; but let us say instead, "you must obey and you can obey, because you are redeemed."

I use redemption here, of course, in the simple sense of being translated out of the kingdom of Satan into the kingdom of God's dear Son and beginning the life in that kingdom; and not in the sense of the full salvation from sin that is to follow. The redemption out of Egypt was only the beginning of the full and grand salvation that awaited the children of Israel further on. But that which followed could not come until this was accomplished. We cannot become followers of God as dear children, until we have first been made "children of God by faith in Christ Jesus."

20 *Then the cloud covered the tent of meeting, and the glory of the Lord filled the tabernacle. (Ex 40:34)*

On the day that the tabernacle was finished the Lord entered in. This coming of the Lord's presence to fill the place prepared for him by his people, is to me a blessed foreshadowing of the baptism of the Holy Spirit, promised by the Lord Jesus to every believer, given first on the day of Pentecost to the waiting disciples whose hearts were prepared for his coming. I believe that to each one of us individually, the command comes now, as it did to the children of Israel then, to prepare a place for our Lord that he may dwell in our midst. I am sure that many have responded to this call, and have known what it is to have the glory of the Lord so fill the house of the Lord, as to leave room for no other inmate. May we all learn this lesson so quickly that we are brought by rapid stages to its consummating glory and know for ourselves this wondrous indwelling!

21 *Pharoah said, "I will let you go, to sacrifice to the Lord your God in the wilderness; only you shall not go very far away." (Ex 8:28)*

When Pharaoh found that he could not induce Moses to remain in the land, he gave up that point, but he added cunningly, "You shall not go very far away." Like Pharaoh, when Satan sees that he cannot keep us in his kingdom, he tries to persuade us that it is not necessary to go very far away and that the world and the church need not be separated by any great distance after all. He knows well, as Pharaoh knew, that it is very easy to take captive those who dwell in the border land, and that it is just because they do not go very far away, that Christians suffer so much from his assaults.

22 *And the flesh of the sacrifice of his peace offerings for thanksgiving shall be eaten on the day of his offering; he shall not leave any of it until the morning. (Lv 7:15)*

In the peace offering the leading thought is the communion of the worshipper. It was not as in the burnt offering, where the sacrifice was enjoyed exclusively by God, but here the worshipper feasted in communion with God. The offering was shared between the altar, the priest, and the offerer.

In New Testament terms, the picture presented to us here is of the believer coming to God to be filled with Christ, to have his thoughts occupied with Christ and his mouth filled with his praises. Many souls have *access* to God who do not have *communion.* They come full of themselves and their own needs, and all they have to say is about their feelings, their sins, or their trials. It is all self, self, self. But communion means to dwell upon and delight in that which God dwells upon and delights in. And this can never be anything in or about ourselves, but always and only things pertaining to his well-beloved Son.

23 *And Aaron shall lay both his hands upon the head of the live goat, and confess over him all the iniquities of the people of Israel, and all their transgressions, all their sins. . . . The goat shall bear all their iniquities upon him to a solitary land.* (Lv 16:21-22)

Of all the types of the Lord Jesus, this seems to me one of the most wonderful. The way of access for the sinner into the presence of God is made by his death, and the sins of the sinner are borne away "into a solitary land," cast as it were into the very depths of the sea, to be no more remembered, even by the God against whom they were committed, but who has thus "laid on him the iniquity of us all."

24 *And being found in human form he humbled himself and became obedient unto death, even death on a cross.* (Phil 2:8)

The cross in connection with Christ always means the death of Christ. The only use of the cross is to put to death, not to keep alive. It may be a suffering death, but it is still sooner or later death. All through the Bible the meaning of the cross is simply and always death. In most cases this is manifest to every one. Why we have chosen to give it a different meaning in its mystical sense and make it mean not death, but a living in misery, would be hard to explain. When, therefore, our Lord told his disciples that they could not be his disciples unless they took up the cross, he could not have meant that they were to find it hard to do his will; but he was, I believe, simply expressing in figurative language the fact that they were to be made partakers of his death and resurrection, by having the old man crucified with him and by living only in the new man, or, in other words, in the resurrection life of the Spirit.

25 *If you obey the voice of the Lord your God, being careful to do all his commandments which I command you this day, the Lord your God will set you high above all the nations of the earth.... But if you will not obey the voice of the Lord your God ... then all these curses shall come upon you and overtake you.* (Dt 28:1, 15)

In Deuteronomy, we meet continually with the word "if." The blessings of the gospel of the Lord Jesus Christ are so unconditional and his gifts are so free, that we are apt to think there are no "ifs" to be found in it anywhere and that the introduction of any conditions is always a mistake of legality. But while it is true that forgiveness is a free gift, bestowed without money and without price upon all who need it and will take it, it is also equally true that holiness of heart is a gift with conditions. No sick man *can* be healed by a physician, no matter how skilled, unless he will submit himself to that physician's prescriptions and obey his orders. And no soul *can* be cured of the dreadful malady of sin, until it is willing to surrender every sin and submit itself to the Lord's commands against it. Conditions do necessarily come in here. Obedience to law has its inevitable blessings, and disobedience its inevitable curses. And the consecration set forth in Deuteronomy is not a legal demand of so much surrender for so much blessing, but it is simply the necessary state in which blessing can be bestowed.

26 *Whenever the cloud was taken up from over the tent, after that the people of Israel set out; and in the place where the cloud settled down, there the people of Israel encamped.* (Nm 9:17)

The presence of the pillar of cloud and fire, guiding and protecting the children of Israel in all their journeys (9:15-23), seems to me a very beautiful type of the presence of the Holy Spirit in the hearts of God's people, guiding them day by day in all the journey of life. There were no roads or guideposts in that great and terrible wilderness and no one who could tell them the way. Yet they journeyed "without carefulness," because the Lord led them at every step. They had none of the care or responsibility of the journey. They had no need to meet and consult about the best paths to take or to send out scouts to choose their route. They had only to watch the pillar of fire and cloud and follow its movements, and all was well. This is a beautiful picture of the believer's absolute dependence upon the blessed guidance of the Holy Spirit and of what ought to be his complete subjection to it.

27

We know that our old self was crucified with him so that the sinful body might be destroyed, and we might no longer be enslaved to sin. (Rom 6:6)

Many people seem to think that the only thing proposed in Christianity is to improve the "old man," i.e., the flesh, and that the way to do this is to discipline and punish it until it is compelled to behave. Hence comes the asceticism of the Buddhist and others; and hence, also, comes the idea that the "cross" for Christians consists in the painful struggles of this helpless "old man" to do the will of God, a will which in the very nature of things the flesh cannot understand or love. But a true comprehension of the religion of Christ shows us that what is really meant is the death of this old man and the birth in us of a "new creature," begotten of God, whose tastes and instincts are all in harmony with God, and to whom the doing of God's will must be, and cannot help being, a joy and a delight. It is not the old man thwarted and made miserable by being compelled to submit to a will it dislikes, but it is a new man, "created in Christ Jesus unto good works," and therefore doing these good works with ease and pleasure—a new nature, of divine origin, which is in harmony with the divine will, and therefore delights to do it.

28 *When I was a child, I spoke like a child, I thought like a child, I reasoned like a child; when I became a man, I gave up childish ways.* (1 Cor 13:11)

The resurrection life is a matter of faith and development. We trust God for it, and he develops it in us. How do people get delivered from the foolishness of childhood? Not by being commanded to give it up, but by growing out of it. When I was a child, I used to think that grown-up people wanted to play as much as I did, only there was a law against it. I thought this law came into effect at a certain age, and I pitied all the people who had reached this age and dreaded growing old myself, because the sad time was drawing nearer for me. But when I had reached maturity, I found there was no law needed, for the desire to play was gone; I had outgrown childish things.

29 *Now Joseph had a dream, and when he told it to his brothers they only hated him the more. He said to them. . . . "Behold, we were binding sheaves in the field, and lo, my sheaf arose and stood upright; and behold, your sheaves gathered round it, and bowed down to my sheaf."* (Gn 37:5-7)

Joseph is a wonderful type of the resurrection life. It is a life which, from the first, dreams of victory and dominion over the things of time and sense; but which can only attain this dominion through suffering. In a dream God revealed Joseph's future kingship to him.

His brethren hated him and called him a "dreamer." And souls that have had a sight of this resurrection life and venture to speak of it will often be hated also and called "mystics" and "dreamers"; and perhaps not even their brethren in the church will understand them.

Joseph's exaltation and victory were sure to come, for God had declared it; but the road to them was by the way of trial, and suffering, and loss. It led through the pit, and through slavery, and through imprisonment in Egypt.

Through emptying to fullness, through abasement to exaltation, is always the way in this resurrection life. This is a necessity in the very nature of things.

If the butterfly life is to be born, the caterpillar life must die. The flesh of man must be put to death, if the spirit of man is to live. This is the explanation of the trial and suffering and loss that come to us all as we advance in the divine life.

Joseph's exaltation came at last, and the only road which could have brought him there was through the very trials that had seemed as if they must crush him. God was in them all and made out of each a chariot to carry him onward.

30 *With whom was [God] provoked forty years? Was it not with those who sinned, whose bodies fell in the wilderness? And to whom did he swear that they should never enter his rest, but to those who were disobedient? So we see that they were unable to enter because of unbelief.* (Heb 3:17-19)

The New Testament tells us that the cause of the sad failure of the Israelites was unbelief. It was not their own weakness nor the strength of their enemies that hindered their entrance. They were, it is true, "grasshoppers," and their enemies were "giants," and it was indeed manifest that they were not able to overcome. But the Lord was able. And he it was who was to fight for them and bring them in.

Their enemies were as great and they themselves were as weak when they crossed the Red Sea. But God delivered them then. No giants or walled cities can successfully oppose God. It was unbelief, therefore, and unbelief alone that prevented their going in.

For the Lord our God who goes before us, he it is who is to fight for us, and is to bring us in, and plant us in the land of our inheritance. Without him we can do absolutely nothing. With him we can do all things. If we depend on him, we will always be "more than conquerors" over every enemy. He has blessed us, he declared, "with all spiritual blessings in heavenly places in Christ," and it only remains for us by faith to go up and possess them. If we do not, it will not be because of our weakness or the strength of our enemies, but because of unbelief. It will be because we measure our enemies with ourselves, instead of measuring them with the Lord. We may be, and indeed are, "grasshoppers" in their sight, but what are they in the sight of God? Truly by the greatness of God's arm they shall all be as nothing before the soul that dares to step out on his promises and trust all to him.

31 *We remember the fish we ate in Egypt for nothing, the cucumbers, the melons, the leeks, the onions, and the garlic; but now our strength is dried up, and there is nothing at all but this manna to look at. (Nm 11:6)*

Almost at once the evil heart of unbelief showed itself, and the people complained. Seduced by the mixed multitude who accompanied them, the Israelites began to look back longingly to Egypt.

The soul that begins by complaining, soon ends by something worse. It loses its relish for heavenly food and looks back with longing to that which the world gives. And the end is sadly typified by the words of Psalm 106: "He gave them what they asked, / but sent a wasting disease among them."

April

1

*I have seen the affliction of my people who are in Egypt. . . .
and I have come down to deliver them out of the hand of
the Egyptians, and to bring them up out of that land to a good
and broad land.* (Ex 3:7-8)

The deliverance of the chosen people from Egypt is a
wonderful picture of the stages by which we are brought to
know the redemption that is in Christ Jesus. We seek first of all
to redeem ourselves by our own efforts, resolutions, and
continual fresh starts, but our failures only grow worse and
worse, until at last we find ourselves in apparently hopeless
bondage. When all hope in ourselves is gone and our bondage
has become very bitter to us, we cry to the Lord, and he hears and
delivers us, and our Exodus is accomplished.

The way of our deliverance is wonderfully pictured in this
story of the deliverance of the children of Israel. From beginning
to end it was God's work, not theirs. His right hand and his
mighty power alone got the victory, and he brought them forth
"with an outstretched arm, and with great terribleness, and with
signs and wonders." They were helpless before the power of

Pharaoh, their cruel master, just as we are helpless before the power of our master, Satan, who has bound us in a far worse slavery than theirs and is even more determined than Pharaoh was, not to let us go. Their helplessness was their greatest claim. Like us, they did not merit redemption, but they needed it; and the Lord delivered them, not because they were worthy, but because he loved them.

2 *The blood shall be a sign for you, upon the houses where you are; and when I see the blood, I will pass over you, and no plague shall fall upon you to destroy you, when I smite the land of Egypt.* (Ex 12:13)

It brings great comfort to my soul to consider the perfect safety of those who belonged to God and stayed in their blood-sprinkled houses while the angel of the Lord "passed over." There were no "ifs" or "buts" in the hearts of those Israelites but perfect assurance of safety. "I will pass over you," was God's word, and they believed it and were at peace. And to us this same word is expressed over and over again in a hundred different ways. Let us then believe him as simply as they did, and our assurance will be as undoubting as theirs.

3 *"For thy sake we are being killed all the day long; / we are regarded as sheep to be slaughtered." / No, in all these things we are more than conquerors through him who loved us.* (Rom 8:36-37)

It is only the resurrection life that can be "more than conqueror" in a world like this. And who would not willingly and gladly lose his own self-life in order to find such an all-conquering life as this?

Consent then to die. Do not seek to improve or make more beautiful the caterpillar life, for no amount of beauty or improvement can turn the caterpillar into the butterfly. The transition can only come through death. Let the old self-life die then, that the new and risen life, the life which is hid with Christ in God, may have free scope to grow and develop. For thus and thus only shall you be able practically and triumphantly to be raised as Christ was raised, to live a new life.

4 *Say to the people of Israel, If any man of you or of your descendants is unclean through touching a dead body, or is afar off on a journey, he shall still keep the Passover of the Lord.*
(Nm 9:10)

The Passover was the memorial of the Israelites' redemption out of Egypt and was to be kept by the people, even in the wilderness. It is a type, I think, of the continual remembrance on our part of the fact that we *have* been redeemed, even though we may know ourselves to be wandering in wilderness places. Neither defilement nor distance was to hinder the keeping of the Passover. But it was to be kept in the second month, instead of the first, teaching that defilement hinders or delays assurance, although it does not deprive the soul of its right to it. A child may be naughty, but it will be still a child, and no parent would be pleased to have it begin to consider itself no longer a child.

5 *Blessed be the God and Father of our Lord Jesus Christ! By his great mercy we have been born anew to a living hope through the resurrection of Jesus Christ from the dead.* (1 Pt 1:3)

Nothing could be more plainly stated. Our spiritual life is born through the resurrection of Jesus Christ. Therefore it has its source in him and derives its nature from him. I am convinced very few of us realize this as a fact. Why else do we struggle so hard to give birth to spiritual life by our own efforts? We try by wrestlings, and agonizings, and resolutions, and religious exercises of all sorts to bring about the "new birth." No wonder religion has become such a hard and apparently hopeless task for so many. Even on the natural plane, the creation of life is a blank impossibility, and how much more on the spiritual plane. The soul, therefore, that tries by its own self-efforts to create spiritual life in itself, is attempting an impossible task and can land itself nowhere but in despair.

6 Jesus answered, "Truly, truly, I say to you, unless one is born of water and the Spirit, he cannot enter the kingdom of God." (Jn 3:5)

John alone, of all the Evangelists, records the sayings of our Lord, introduced by the words, "Truly, truly." (There are twenty-four of these sayings in his Gospel, and all of them develop the laws of the spiritual life.) This "Truly, truly" states the incontrovertible fact that the only way into any form of life is to be born into it. Things grow *in* a life, but they cannot grow *into* it. The doorway into any plane of life is always by birth.

7 But God, who is rich in mercy, out of the great love with which he loved us, even when we were dead through our trespasses, made us alive together with Christ (by grace you have been saved). (Eph 2:4-5)

The divine seed within us is being quickened by the Holy Spirit whenever we feel inward stirrings and longings after holiness. This is the begetting of God. Then comes our responsibility. We cannot create life, but we can let life live. We can lay hold of it by an entire surrender to Christ, who is our life. We can accept him as our life and refuse to let any other life live in us. We can reckon ourselves to be alive in him.

8 A man is not justified by works of the law but through faith in Jesus Christ. (Gal 2:16)

This, then, is how the spiritual life is to grow; that is, by surrender and faith. We must boycott the old self-life and must deal only with the spiritual life. But we must not make another mistake and think that although we cannot beget life by our self-efforts, we are to make it grow ourselves. We are as powerless in the matter of our growth as in the matter of our begetting. Life grows of itself. It is a mighty dynamic force that only asks a chance to grow.

9 *Do not labor for the food which perishes, but for the food which endures to eternal life, which the Son of man will give to you. . . . I am the bread of life; he who comes to me shall not hunger, and he who believes in me shall never thirst.*

(Jn 6:27, 35)

Christians are continually trying to feed their spiritual life with all sorts of things other than Christ. They feed on the dry husks of dogmas and doctrines, or on forms and ceremonies, or on religious duties well performed, or on Christian work of various kinds, or on good resolutions, or on fervent emotions; and then they wonder at their starved condition. Nothing can really satisfy the hunger of the soul but Christ. To draw our life from Christ means to be so united to his nature that the same spiritual life flows through our spiritual veins that flowed through his. This subject is often regarded as mystical and difficult to understand. But there is a practical way of looking at the matter that seems to me simple and easy to understand. We feed ourselves on the writings of a great author by becoming familiar with them and by adopting their teachings as our own; and in the same way we must feed on Christ. We know what it is to become one in thought and feeling with a well-loved and honored friend and to share that friend's inmost life; similarly we must become one with Christ. We can understand how an artist can feed his mind on the life and work and teaching of some great master in art and so become like him, able to follow in that master's footsteps; and just so must we do with Christ.

10 *You did not choose me, but I chose you and appointed you that you should go and bear fruit and that your fruit should abide.* (Jn 15:16)

A living plant always bears fruit. It is the law of its life that it should do so; and it is equally a law that this fruit should come, not by effort, but by spontaneous growth.

We need not trouble ourselves about our fruit-bearing. It is "appointed" that we shall bring it forth, just as it is appointed that a fig tree shall bear figs. It is the law of our spiritual life; and we can no more have real spiritual life within us without bearing fruit than the oak tree can have life without bearing acorns. Very few seem to understand this. As a consequence, there is a vast amount of effort among Christians to hang fruit onto their branches by some outside performances of one sort or another. It is as though a man bought apples and hung them on his apple trees in order to secure a good crop of fruit! Fruit must be "brought forth," not fastened on. This is the law of fruit-bearing, and to try to violate this law can only bring confusion and death.

11
Can a fig tree, my brethren, yield olives, or a grapevine figs? No more can salt water yield fresh. (Jas 3:12)

Another one of the laws of life is that all plants must yield fruit after their own kind. I must be content, therefore, to be just the species of plant and to bear just the kind of fruit that the Divine Husbandman pleases. We do not always find that we like to be what God has made us to be. Perhaps I would like to be a rosebush and blossom out in roses, when he has made me a potato plant and wants me to yield potatoes. I might be tempted to get paper roses and sew them on. But what folly! A million paper roses could not turn my potato plant into a rosebush, and the first person who tried to pick one would find me out! All that I need to do is to see to it that, whatever species of plant I may be, I become a healthy vigorous plant and fulfill the law of my being without grumbling. Be content to be what your God has made you, but do not be content until you are the best of its kind.

12 *But he said to me, "My grace is sufficient for you, for my power is made perfect in weakness." I will all the more gladly boast of my weaknesses, that the power of Christ may rest upon me. (2 Cor 12:9)*

The law of the spiritual life is that divine strength will be made perfect in human weakness. Our part is to supply the weakness; God's part is to supply the strength. We are, however, continually trying to usurp God's part and to supply the strength ourselves. Because we cannot do this, we are plunged into depths of discouragement. We think that in order to work effectively for the Lord we ought to feel strong in ourselves. When instead we find ourselves feeling weak, we are in despair. But the Bible teaches us that, if we only knew it, our weakness is in reality our greatest strength.

13 *But we have this treasure in earthen vessels, to show that the transcendent power belongs to God and not to us. (2 Cor 4:7)*

It is of vital importance to the children of God that they should understand the law that God's strength can be made perfect only in human weakness. For in the spiritual life the natural man never can feel strong in itself, and if we think it ought to, we shall be continually troubled. However, if we understand this law, we shall learn, like Paul, to take pleasure in our infirmities and our weaknesses, because we shall see that only when we are weak are we really spiritually strong.

The choice lies between the strength of our own human nature and the strength of the divine nature within us. To the tiny unquickened mustard seed the weight of earth above it could not but seem like an immovable mountain; but, when quickened, the life within that same tiny seed pushes aside those mountains of earth without any apparent effort. Life carries all before it, and no obstacles can withstand its progress. Even rocks are upheaved by the irresistible power of life in a tiny creeper. It is life, more life that we want, not more effort.

14   *I came that they may have life, and have it abundantly.*
                                (Jn 10:10)

Every plant has its own laws of life and can only flourish in certain localities and under certain conditions of soil and climate. This is equally true of the spiritual life. Even so, outward localities and outward climate make no difference here, although Christians often seem to think they do. We find ourselves in uncongenial surroundings and are tempted to think our spiritual life cannot flourish in such environments. But no outward circumstances can affect the life of the soul. Its true environment is all inward and spiritual; and this environment is none other than God and his love. "For you are dead, and your life is hid with Christ in God." The sources of one's life, that is, the objects and aims and underlying springs of action, must be either in the self or in God. If in the self, then our life is hid in self; if in God, then our life is hid in God; and to "dwell in God" or to "abide in Christ" mean simply that we have the underlying spring of all our thoughts, words, and actions in him.

15   *For God alone my soul waits in silence; / from him*
      comes my salvation. (Ps 62:1)

The whole *theory* of wise conduct may be summed up in the knowledge of when to act and when to refrain from action; the whole *practice* consists in acting according to such knowledge. A complete mastery of both theory and practice is rarely attained by an individual, but that is no reason why we should not try to attain it. "Surely," many persons may exclaim, "it cannot require much intelligence to wait." On the contrary, it is often a very difficult thing to do nothing *judiciously*; or, in other words, it is often a greater trial to a man's spirit to *wait* than to *work.* How often are we placed in circumstances which no action of our own is likely to improve—in which it is clearly prudent to take no step, to do nothing, to say nothing; but to wait and see what the opposite party will do or say. Restless from temperament or some other cause, people go and do something when it would be infinitely better if they had sat quietly at home and done nothing. How frequently are clever people the victims of this overactivity! All cultivated persons are aware of the importance of work, but few have considered how much wisdom there often is in waiting. Of all the lessons that humanity has to learn in life's school, the hardest is to learn to wait.

16 *Love does no wrong to a neighbor; therefore love is the fulfilling of the law.* (Rom 13:10)

This is the most essential law of love, that characteristic which makes it inclusive of all other laws, namely, "love does no wrong to its neighbor," knowing it to be wrong. For love to do wrong is as impossible as for the sun to give darkness instead of light. Love loves and cannot, therefore, do anything contrary to love. It is not that it will not or ought not, but simply and only that it *cannot*. It is an inevitable law.

We must remember, however, that a great deal of what is called love ought really to be spelled s-e-l-f-i-s-h-n-e-s-s. People love their own enjoyment of their friends more than they love the friends themselves, and consider their own welfare in their intercourse with those they profess to love, far more than the welfare of the so-called loved ones. It has been said that we never really love anyone until we can do without them for their good. How many lives are marred and made miserable by the selfishness of some relative or friend (too often a parent), who, under the plea of love, will not allow the least liberty of action on the part of their loved ones. They will do everything possible to hinder their development in every line that is not agreeable to themselves. Surely such a course, however it may be disguised, can spring from nothing but selfishness.

17 *Beloved, let us love one another; for love is of God, and he who loves is born of God and knows God. He who does not love does not know God; for God is love.* (1 Jn 4:7-8)

God is love; therefore love is the key to the mystery of God. He is not only loving, but he is infinitely more than that; he is love itself. The sun not only gives light, but it is light, the source, center, and very being of light itself. This is always the case, even though the fact may be hidden from our eyes by clouds or misrepresented by colored or smoked glass.

We have all used the expression "God is love" hundreds of times, no doubt; but I am afraid it has conveyed to our minds no real idea of the facts of the case.

If we would know God, we must know what love is; and then we must apply to God all the best and highest that we know of love. For God is absolutely under the law of love; that is, he is under an inevitable constraint to obey it. He alone of all the universe, because his very essence or nature is love, cannot help loving. We, alas! whose natures are not altogether composed of love, but are mixed up with a great many other things, can help loving and very often do help it. Because this is the case with ourselves, we think it must also be the case with him; and we torment ourselves with imagining that, because of our own unworthiness, he will surely fail to love us. What a useless torment it is! How little real sense there is in it!

18   *Why, one will hardly die for a righteous man—though perhaps for a good man one will dare even to die. But God shows his love for us in that while we were yet sinners Christ died for us. (Rom 5:7-8)*

One of the laws of love is that it loves for love's sake only and not because of anything lovable in the object. How often we have seen mothers lavishing a wealth of love upon children who did not seem to others to possess one single lovable quality. One of my children once said to me, in a fit of remorse after a spell of bad behavior, "Oh, mother I do not see how you *can* love such a naughty little girl as I am." And I replied, "Ah, darling, you cannot understand. I do not love you for what you are, but I love you for what I am. I am your mother, and I love you because of

my mother-heart of love; I should love you just the same no
matter what you did. I should not love your bad behavior, but I
should love you."

19 *But if you hearken attentively to his voice, and do all
that I say, then I will be an enemy to your enemies, and
an adversary to your adversaries.* (Ex 23:22)

Obedience is the logical outcome of yielding and trusting. If I
yield myself up into the care of a physician and trust him to cure
me, I must necessarily obey his orders. If I am lost in a
wilderness and surrender myself to the care of a guide, I must
walk in the paths he points out. No guide can lead a lost traveler
home, if that traveler refuses to follow his guidance and persists
in walking in paths he forbids. If we want the Lord to care for us,
and protect us from our enemies, and provide for our needs, it
stands to reason that we must obey his voice and walk in the
paths he marks out for us.

20 *Joseph said to them ... "You meant evil against me; but
God meant it for good, to bring it about that many
people should be kept alive, as they are today."* (Gn 50:19-20)

This is the secret of all those trials which come to us from the
wrath or malice of men. They think evil against us, perhaps, but
God means it for good; and we can therefore say with Joseph, of
each one, "It was not you" who did it, "but God."

Knowing this, it is not strange that the Apostle should assert
so triumphantly his deliverance from all fear of what man can
do to him. "For He has said, 'I will never fail you nor forsake you.'
Hence we can confidently say, 'The Lord is my helper, / I will not
be afraid; / what can man do to me?'" (Heb 13:5-6).

The death of our Lord Jesus Christ on the cross was another
illustration of this truth. It certainly was by wicked hands that
he was crucified and slain; and yet these "wicked hands" only
accomplished, all unconsciously to themselves, God's plan for
the salvation of the world.

21   *Behold, I set before you this day a blessing and a curse:*
      the blessing, if you obey the commandments of the
Lord your God, which I command you this day, and the curse, if
you do not obey the commandments of the Lord your God, but
turn aside from the way which I command you this day, to go
after other gods which you have not known. (Dt 11:26-28)

Obedience may be said to be simply a matter of self-interest. It
is not a demand made of us, but a privilege offered. Like yielding
and trusting, it is simply a way of bringing divine wisdom and
power to bear upon our affairs. If we could only learn to look
upon it in this commonsense kind of way, we should find that it
had lost half of its terrors. We should be able to say then with
our Divine Master, "I delight to do your will," and not merely I
consent to do it.

A great many people *consent* to obey God because they are
afraid of the consequences of disobedience, but they find no
delight in it. If, however, they would only look for a little while
on the other side and see something of the unspeakably blessed
consequences of obedience, they would find themselves de-
lighting in obedience, and even embracing it eagerly, and
rejoicing in the privilege of it.

22   *And the kingdom and the dominion/and the greatness*
      of the kingdoms under the whole heaven / shall be
given to the people of the saints of the Most High; / their
kingdom shall be an everlasting kingdom, / and all dominions
shall serve and obey them. (Dn 7:27)

How few of the children of God have realized their true
position in this universal kingdom and dominion of the Son of
Man! It is our birthright to find all things made our servants, but
instead we allow most things to become our masters. A trial
comes, or a disappointment, and instead of recognizing it as
God's servant, sent to bring us some blessing from his hand, we
bow down to it as our tyrannical master and let it crush us into

darkness and despair. How then should God's servants be received?

Since all things are God's servants, all things must necessarily be his messengers, and therefore every event of life has its message for us. Many of our choicest gifts come to us by the hands of very rough-looking messengers and are wrapped up in coarse brown packages. My neighbor who treats me unkindly, or my friend who wrongs me, or my enemy who maligns me, have a message from God for me as truly as the pastor who preaches to me or as the Christian friend who gives me a tract. We little know the rich blessing we lose because we despise and misuse the "servants" who bring them. Perhaps the gift of patience, for which you have prayed long and apparently in vain, is held in the hand of that very disagreeable inmate of your household, whose presence has seemed to you such an unkind infliction. Or it may be that the victory over the world, for which your soul has fervently hungered, was shut up in that very disappointment or loss, against which you have rebelled with such bitterness.

23 *Then his [Job's] wife said to him, "Do you still hold fast your integrity? Curse God, and die." But he said to her, "You speak as one of the foolish women would speak. Shall we receive good at the hand of God, and shall we not receive evil?" In all this Job did not sin with his lips. (Jb 2:9-10)*

In the story of Job we have a very striking illustration of trust in God. All sorts of misfortunes came upon him, originated by all sorts of agencies. His oxen and his asses were stolen by the Sabeans; his sheep and his servants were burned up by lightning; his camels were carried away by the Chaldeans; his sons and his daughters were crushed by the collapse of the house where they were feasting; and finally Job himself was afflicted with painful boils from the crown of his head to the sole of his foot. There were very different instruments employed in bringing these misfortunes to pass, and yet all of them—Satan, the Sabeans, the lightning, the Chaldeans, the great wind from the wilderness, and the boils that covered Job's body—all were God's ways of accomplishing his blessed purpose of maturing the fruits of meekness, and patience, and submission, and trust, in the heart of Job, and of bringing him into greater nearness and communion with himself at last.

Job evidently received these afflictions from the hand of God, for he took no notice in any case of the "second causes," but referred his trials right back to God. "The Lord gave," he said, "and the Lord has taken away: blessed be the name of the Lord."

24 *Whatever the Lord pleases he does, / in heaven and on earth, / in the seas and all deeps.* (Ps 135:6)

If God "pleases" to let me undergo a trial, he has in that act adopted my trial as his servant to accomplish his will in my life.

One of the greatest difficulties in the Christian life arises from the failure to see this fact. The child of God says, "It would be easy to say 'Thy will be done' to my trials, if I could only see that they come from God. But *my* trials and crosses come almost always from some human hand, and I cannot say 'Thy will be done' to human beings." This is all true; but what if we should see, in every human instrument only one of God's "servants," coming to us with hands full of messages and blessing from him? Could we not then receive them with submission and even with thankfulness? The trial itself may be very hard for flesh and blood to bear, and I do not mean that we can be thankful for that, but the blessing it brings is surely always cause for the deepest thankfulness. I may not be able to give thanks for an unkind friend, but I can give thanks for the patience and meekness brought to me through the instrument of this friend's unkindness.

25 *Rejoice always, pray constantly, give thanks in all circumstances; for this is the will of God in Christ Jesus for you.* (1 Thes 5:16-18)

No one can possibly obey this command to give thanks in everything, who fails to see that everything works to the good for those who love God. In truth, every event of life, even the most disagreeable, is only a bearer of blessing; and as a consequence, all the days of such who believe are filled with continual thanksgiving.

Perhaps some may ask why it is, if all things are indeed God's servants sent to bring us some message or some gift, that they themselves never seem to get these gifts or messages. The answer is simply this, that because these gifts and messages have come to them wrapped in coarse and ugly packages, they have refused to receive and open them. Their ears have been so filled with their own complainings, that they could not hear God's message, and their eyes have been so absorbed in looking at the seen suffering and hardness that they fail to look for the unseen blessing.

It makes the best sense, therefore, to welcome every event of life as God's servant, bringing us something from him; and to overlook the unattractiveness of the messenger in the joy of the message, and forget the hurt of the trial in the sweetness of the blessing it brings.

26 *A thorn was given me in the flesh, a messenger of Satan, to harass me, to keep me from being too elated. Three times I besought the Lord about this, that it should leave me; but he said to me, "My grace is sufficient for you, for my power is made perfect in weakness." I will all the more gladly boast of my weaknesses, that the power of Christ may rest upon me.... for when I am weak, then I am strong.* (2 Cor 12:7-10)

Paul had learned to "boast" of his weakness and to accept the fact that a "messenger of Satan" was sent to "harass him." Nothing could possibly have a worse origin than a "messenger of Satan," and nothing would seem at first sight to be less like a tool or a servant of God; and yet Paul evidently recognized it as such, and was thankful for it, because he found that shut up in this very "thorn in the flesh" was the blessed revelation to his soul of the power of Christ resting upon him. For the sake of a similar revelation, who would not welcome a similar thorn!

27 *For God is at work in you, both to will and to work for his good pleasure.* (Phil 2:13)

Our will is a piece of splendid equipment, a sort of rudder, such as they have on sailboats to direct the course of the boat; and everything depends upon the intelligence that guides its action; whether it is guided by our ignorance or by God's wisdom. As long as our own ignorance is the guide, the boat is sure to go astray, and it is dangerous for us to say, "I will" or "I will not." But when we have surrendered our wills to God and are letting him "work in us to will and to work for his good pleasure," we are then called upon to set our faces like a flint to carry out his will and must respond with an emphatic "I will" to every "Thou shalt" of his.

28 *My food is to do the will of him who sent me, and to accomplish his work.* (Jn 4:34)

Your attitude towards God is as real when only the will acts, as when every emotion seems to support your choice. It may not seem as real to us, but in God's sight it is as real and often, I think, all the more real, because we are unencumbered by a lot of unmanageable feelings. When, therefore, this wretched feeling of unreality or hypocrisy comes, do not be troubled by it. It is only in the region of your emotions and means nothing, except perhaps that your digestion is out of order, or that there is an east wind blowing. Simply see to it that your will is in God's hands; that your true inward personality is abandoned to his working; that your choice, your decision, is on his side; and leave it there. Your surging emotions, like a tossing vessel which by degrees yields to the steady pull of the anchor, will find themselves attached to the mighty power of God by the choice of your will. They must inevitably come around. It is a psychological fact, not generally known, that our will can control our feelings, if only we are "steadfastly minded." Many times, when my feelings have declared unmistakably that I was going in a direction contrary to the facts, I have changed those feelings by a steadfast assertion of their opposite. Similarly, I have been able many times to control my rebellious feelings against the will of God by steadfast assertions of my choice to accept and submit to his will. Sometimes it has seemed to drain me of all the willpower I possessed to say, "Thy will be done," so contrary has it been to the evidence of my senses or my emotions. But invariably, sooner or later, the victory has come. God has taken possession of the will thus surrendered to him and has worked in me to will and to do of his good pleasure.

29 *Let each of you look not only to his own interests but also to the interests of others. Have this mind among yourselves, which is yours in Christ Jesus, who, though he was in the form of God, did not count equality with God a thing to be grasped.... Therefore God has highly exalted him and bestowed on him the name which is above every name. (Phil 2:4-6, 9)*

Lowliness of mind is the only true road to honor. He that humbles himself shall be exalted and no one else. Our divine Master has set us this example; and if we really want to have the "mind that was in Christ Jesus," we must be willing to be made of no reputation and must take, not the place of mastery, but the place of service.

30 *Finally, my brethren, rejoice in the Lord. (Phil 3:1)*

The consummation of all Christian experience is to bring the soul to the place where it has learned how to "rejoice in the Lord" and to be satisfied in him alone. "Finally, my brethren," Paul says, or, in other words, "The summing up, my brethren, of all I have to say to you is simply this, rejoice in the Lord." Probably, if we had written the epistles, we would have given very different advice. We would have said, "Finally, my brethren, rejoice in your faithfulness; or, rejoice in your wonderful experiences; or, rejoice in your hard work for the Lord; or, rejoice in your growth in grace." We would almost certainly have been rejoicing in something about ourselves. Yet any rejoicing which has self for its foundation must necessarily end in disappointment, for sooner or later self always disappoints us, no matter how good or even how pious a self it may be.

May

1 *Take my yoke upon you, and learn from me; for I am gentle and lowly in heart, and you will find rest for your souls.*
(Mt 11:29)

To be "gentle and lowly in heart" one must get rid of the ME. Some people think they are humble and lowly in heart when they say bitter and disparaging things about themselves, but I am convinced that the giant ME is often quite as much exalted and puffed up by self-blame as by self-praise. The simple truth is that we ought not to think or talk about our ME at all. Self is so greedy of notice that it would rather be blamed than not noticed at all. This seems strange, but I believe the reason is that self feels as if the very saying, "I am so bad," proves that it is not so very bad after all, since it can be so humble! It is, however, a very different thing to say disparaging things about ourselves than to have someone else say them about us. Think for a moment how you would feel if your friends were to agree with such remarks and were to repeat them to others as their own opinions. Suppose the next time you said, "Oh, I am such a poor good-for-nothing creature," someone should reply, "Yes, that is exactly what I have always thought about you." How would your ME like that? The truth is our ME always expects the disparaging remarks it makes about itself to be denied; and it often, even if unconsciously, makes them for the express purpose of having them denied, and of having its humility admired and applauded. What can be more delicious to a delicate self-love than to hear itself applauded for having none! The truly meek and lowly heart does not want to talk about ME at all, either for good or evil. It wants to forget its very existence. As Fenelon writes, it says to this ME, "I do not know you, and am not interested in you. You are a stranger to me, and I do not care what happens to you nor how you are treated." If people slight you or treat you with neglect, the meek and lowly heart accepts all as its rightful portion. True humility makes us love to be treated, both by God and man, as we feel our imperfections really deserve; and, instead of resenting such treatment, we welcome it and are thankful for it.

2 *And you shall remember all the way which the Lord your God has led you these forty years in the wilderness, that he might humble you, testing you to know what was in your heart, whether you would keep his commandments, or not. And he humbled you and let you hunger and fed you with manna.*

(Dt 8:2-3)

Many of us may be at this moment taking the same sort of medicine that the Lord was obliged to give to the children of Israel. We need, perhaps, to be "humbled," as much as they did, that we may not be tempted to say in our hearts, "My power and the might of my hand has gotten me this wealth." The Lord is therefore obliged to "let us hunger" and to "lead us through the wildernesses" to test us and to humble us. Should this be our experience, we must look at the blessed cure to be wrought and take our medicine, no matter how bitter may be its taste, with cheerful and thankful hearts.

The Apostle Paul understood the true commonsense of humility. He tells the Philippians the causes he had for self-glorification but declares that he "counted all these things but dung," so worthless had he discovered them to be. He bids good-bye to his own gigantic ME, and cries out in language I wish we could all adopt, "I am crucified with Christ; it is no longer I who live, but Christ who lives in me" (Gal 2:20).

3 I have been crucified with Christ; it is no longer I who live, but Christ who lives in me; and the life I now live in the flesh I live by faith in the Son of God, who loved me and gave himself for me. (Gal 2:20)

This "no longer I" is one of those "swords of the Spirit" about which Paul speaks when he describes the Christian's armor, and I know none that is more effective in our conflict with the unruly giant ME. Not even a giant can resist the disintegrating process of an absolute and persistent resolution to ignore his existence; and if we will but adopt Paul's language, we cannot fail sooner or later to gain Paul's glorious victories.

4 Keep your heart with all vigilance; for from it flow the springs of life. (Prv 4:23)

By whatever name philosophers may call this "heart" out of which flow the "springs of life," commonsense would teach us that it means nothing more or less than the will; for certainly to my consciousness the will is the governing force in my nature and the spring of all my actions. It is out of the secret springs of our will that we bring forth the good or evil treasures of our lives. No one who will take a concordance and run their eyes down the long list of passages concerning the "heart" can fail to see that when God speaks of the "heart," he means something far different than that bundle of emotions which we usually call our hearts. We, too, often use the word heart in a far deeper sense. We speak, for instance, of getting "at the heart" of a matter, and we mean, not the feelings that accompany it, but the central idea that dominates it. In the same way when God speaks of our "hearts," he means our true central self, that "ego" within us that dominates our whole being. The word is used in the Bible more than one thousand times. The heart is said to understand and to be ignorant, to be wise and to be silly, to exercise good judgment or bad, to be stupefied, to grow fat, to resist the light, to be discouraged, to fluctuate in doubt, to be of the same mind with another, to seek knowledge, to work wickedness, to devise wicked imaginations, to be set to do evil, to be set to do good, to be astonished, to tremble, to be glad; it is said, in short, to do and to be exactly what the man himself is said to do and to be. In innumerable instances where the word "heart" is used, it would not make sense to translate it by the affections or the emotions.

5 *Burnt offering and sin offering thou hast not required. / Then I said, "Lo, I come; / in the roll of the book it is written of me; / I delight to do thy will, O my God." (Ps 40:6-7)*

Fenelon says: "I do not ask from you a love that is tender and emotional, but only that your will should lean towards love. The purest of all loves is a will so filled with the will of God that there remains nothing else." We "delight" to do the will of God, not because our piety is so exalted, but because we have the sense to see that his will is the best; and therefore what he wants we want also. This sort of delight may not be as pleasing to ourselves, but it is far more satisfactory to him than any amount of delight in joyous emotions or gratifying luminations.

Someone will ask whether we are not told to give up our wills. To this I answer, yes, but in giving up our wills we are not meant to become empty of willpower, to be left poor, flabby, nerveless creatures who have no will. We are simply meant to substitute for our own foolish, misdirected wills of ignorance and immaturity the perfect and beautiful and wise will of God. It is not willpower in the abstract we are to give up, but our misguided use of that willpower. The will we are to give up is our will as it is misdirected and so parted from God's will, not our will when it is one with God's will. For when our will is in harmony with his will, when it has the stamp of oneness with him, it would be wrong for us to give it up.

6 *Behold, all was vanity and a striving after wind, and there was nothing to be gained under the sun. (Eccl 2:11)*

A little exercise of commonsense would show us that this must be the inevitable result of everything that has ME and ME only for its center. There is never anything to be gained in it, but it is always a grievous loss, and it can never turn out to be anything but "vanity and a striving after the wind" or, as another translation puts it, "vexation of spirit." Have we not all discovered something of this in our own experience? You have set your heart, perhaps, on procuring something for the benefit or pleasure of your own great big ME; but when you have secured it, this ungrateful ME has refused to be satisfied and has turned away from what it has cost you so much to procure. Or you have labored to have the claims of this ME recognized by those around you and have reared with great pains and effort a high pinnacle, upon which you have seated yourself to be admired by all beholders. And lo! at the critical moment, the pinnacle has tottered over, and your glorious ME has fallen into the dust; and contempt, instead of honor, has become its portion. Never, under any circumstances, has it really in the end paid you to try and exalt your great exacting ME, for always, sooner or later, it has all proved to be nothing but vanity and vexation of spirit.

7 *When you are invited by any one to a marriage feast, do not sit down in a place of honor, lest a more eminent man than you be invited. . . . Go and sit in the lowest place, so that when your host comes he may say to you, "Friend, go up higher"; then you will be honored in the presence of all. (Lk 14:8, 10)*

ME is a most exacting person, requiring the best seats and the highest places for itself, and feeling grievously wounded if its claims are not recognized and its rights considered. Most of the quarrels among Christian workers arise from the clamorings of this gigantic ME. "So and so is exalted above ME"; "My rights have been trampled upon"; "No one considers ME." How much there is of this sort of thing, expressed or unexpressed, in every heart where ME is king! How few of us understand the true glory of taking our seats in the lowest rooms! And yet if we are to have real "honor in the presence of all," this is what we must do.

8 *Likewise you that are younger be subject to the elders. Clothe yourselves, all of you, with humility toward one another, for "God opposes the proud, but gives grace to the humble." (1 Pt 5:5)*

It seems very hard for Christians to take on this spirit of subjection to one another. The ME in them rebels mightily at any suggestion of such a thing. And yet in the kingdom of heaven it is the only road to greatness.

Our Lord tells us we do well to beware of people who "love salutations in the market-places, and the chief seats in the synagogues, and the uppermost places at a feast"; and our own instincts tell us the same.

9 *Repent, and be baptized every one of you in the name of Jesus Christ for the forgiveness of your sins; and you shall receive the gift of the Holy Spirit. For the promise is to you and to your children and to all that are far off. (Acts 2:38-39)*

The Holy Spirit, like the sunlight, is free to all. The world is full of sunlight, but the plant in a cellar dwindles and dies for lack of it. What is needed is not a new outpouring of the sunlight, but the placing of the plant in the sunlight which is already poured out. It is not that God must give anything more, but that we must receive more of that which he has already given.

Be filled with that Spirit which fills all the earth around you. Do not ask for more of the Spirit, but let the Spirit have more of you.

10 *Do you not know that your body is a temple of the Holy Spirit within you, which you have from God?*

(1 Cor 6:19)

This is in a sense true of all Christians, for on the day of Pentecost the Holy Spirit came to the church, "which is the house of God," to abide in her midst forever. But in individual experience, the power of it is not always known, and each soul needs to come to its own Pentecost. The conscious presence of the abiding Comforter is not realized by every Christian. All, of course, must have the Spirit, because the new birth is impossible without his presence and power. But to some souls there comes at a certain stage in their progress a wonderful experience, which they seem instinctively to call the baptism of the Holy Spirit, and which lifts them up into a region of spiritual life that is as far above their former level, as the mountain top is above the valley, and from which but few ever descend. This baptism does for souls now, just what it did for the disciples on the day of Pentecost. It purifies; it transforms; it endues with power from on high; it satisfies; it comforts; it inspires; it controls. It bestows upon those who receive it, that "well of water springing up into everlasting life," for the soul's own comfort, and those "rivers of living water" flowing out for the blessing of others, which our Lord promised to all who should believe in him.

11   *Then Ephraim shall become like a mighty warrior, / and their hearts shall be glad as with wine. / Their children shall see it and rejoice, / their hearts shall exult in the Lord.*
(Zc 10:7)

To rejoice in the Lord is not a pious fiction, nor is it merely a religious phrase. Neither is it anything mysterious or awe-inspiring. It is just good plain happiness and comfort. It is something people around us can see and be glad about. It smoothes away the frowns and shuts out the sighs. Long faces and gloomy tones of voice disappear in its presence. It is even full of innocent mirthfulness and lightheartedness. I remember my dear father, who was a saint on earth if ever there was one. Once, during what was considered a very solemn occasion, something struck his sense of the ludicrous, and he gave a merry lighthearted laugh. A friend reproved him for laughing on such a "solemn occasion." He turned to me and said in his dear merry voice, calling me by my pet name, "Han, if people who know their sins are forgiven and that God loves them and cares for them cannot laugh, I don't know who can." I believe I have never since had a good laugh at anything, that it has not recalled to my mind my father's genuine happiness in knowing himself to be in the care and keeping of his Father in heaven.

12 *Then he said to them, "Go your way, eat the fat and drink sweet wine and send portions to him for whom nothing is prepared; for this day is holy to our Lord; and do not be grieved, for the joy of the Lord is your strength." (Neh 8:10)*

Joy is always a source of strength. When we are happy, we feel equal to anything; when we are cast down, everything is a burden. This is true on the earthly plane, and of course it is just as true on the spiritual plane, for the psychological laws that govern the two realms are the same. It seems, however, as if many Christians thought the laws of these two realms were exactly opposite to one another and that depression and discouragement were greater elements of strength in the spiritual life than joy could ever be. Consequently, depression and discouragement are looked upon as very pious and humble frames of mind, and joy is considered to be a sort of spiritual bon-bon, only to be partaken of at rare and uncertain intervals.

13 *Because you did not serve the Lord your God with joyfulness and gladness of heart, by reason of the abundance of all things, therefore you shall serve your enemies whom the Lord will send against you . . . and he will put a yoke of iron upon your neck, until he has destroyed you. (Dt 28:47-48)*

Notice the use of the words "because" and "therefore" in these two passages. "Because" the Lord is not served with joyfulness and gladness, "therefore" there can be no fruit, and service becomes "a yoke of iron" upon our necks. This "because" and "therefore" are inseparably connected in the spiritual life. The "therefore" is not an arbitrary sentence of God, but the natural and necessary result of the "because." If we will not rejoice and be glad in heart in the Lord, then we shall inevitably be in hunger, in thirst, in nakedness, and in want of all things elsewhere. For our souls are of such a divine origin, that no other joy but joy in God can ever satisfy them. It is like trying to satisfy a man of culture with the joys of a savage. He simply could not enjoy them. They would give him no pleasure, but would, instead, bore him and weary him beyond words; and this is why all the joys of earth so soon fade. They cannot satisfy the soul that was made for God.

14 *May those who sow in tears reap with shouts of joy! / He that goes forth weeping, bearing the seed for sowing, / shall come home with shouts of joy, bringing his sheaves with him. (Ps 126:6)*

God who made the soul, made it for this high destiny, and his object, therefore, in all the discipline and training of life, is to bring us to the place where we shall find our joy in him alone. For this purpose he is obliged often to stain our pleasant pictures and to thwart and disappoint our brightest anticipations. He *detaches* us from all else that he may *attach* us to himself; not from an arbitrary will, but because he knows that only so can we be really happy. I do not mean by this that it will be necessary for all one's friends to die, or for all one's money to be lost; but I do mean that the soul shall find itself, either from inward or outward causes, desolate and bereft and empty of all comfort, except in God. We must come to the end of everything that is not God, in order to find our joy in God alone.

15 *Then I will go to the altar of God, to God my exceeding joy; / and I will praise thee with the lyre, O God, my God. (Ps 43:4)*

To "go" to him is nothing mysterious. It simply means to turn our minds to him, to rest our hearts on him, and to turn away

from all other resting places. It means that we must not look at
or think about and trouble over our circumstances, our surroundings, our perplexities, or our experiences. But we must
look at and think about the Lord, and must ask ourselves, not,
"How do I feel about this?" but, "How does the Lord feel?" not,
"How shall I manage it?" but, "How will He manage it?"

16 *But let all who take refuge in thee rejoice, / let them
ever sing for joy;/ and do thou defend them,/ that those
who love thy name may exult in thee.* [Ps 5:11]

___

The Bible is full of declarations concerning rejoicing in the
Lord. In order to fully understand the subject, we must have a
clear comprehension of what spiritual joy and gladness really
are. Some people seem to look upon spiritual joy as a thing, a sort
of lump or package of joy, stored away in one's heart, to be
looked at and rejoiced over. Now, as a fact, joy is not a thing at
all. It is only the gladness that comes from the possession of
something good or the knowledge of something pleasant.
Christian joy is simply our gladness in knowing Christ and in
our possession of such a God and Savior. We do not on an
earthly plane rejoice in our joy, but in the thing that causes our
joy. On the heavenly plane it is the same. We are not to rejoice in
our joy, but we are to "rejoice in the Lord, and joy in the God of
our salvation." And this joy no man or devil can take from us,
and no earthly sorrows can touch.

17 *Then he led forth his people like sheep, / and guided
them in the wilderness like a flock. /He led them in
safety, so that they were not afraid;/ but the sea overwhelmed
their enemies. / And he brought them to his holy land.*

[Ps 78:52-54]

___

One writer says that the spiritual life is divided into three
stages: the stage of joyful beginnings, the stage of desolation,
and the stage of joy in God alone. First, there is the state of
beginnings, when the soul is full of sensible delights and when
everything in our life seems to prosper. Then, as the soul

advances in the divine life, there comes very often the stage of desolation, when the Christian seems to pass through a wilderness, and to suffer, it may be, the loss of all things, both inward and outward. If this period of desolation is faithfully traversed, there comes finally, on the other side of it, the stage of an unaltered and unalterable joy and gladness in God. All has been lost in the desert stage, that all may be found in God further on. The only danger is that the soul in this desert stage might faint and fail under the stress of desolation and turn back to the fleshpots of Egypt for its joy. One writer says that this desert is filled with the bodies of "frustrated saints"; and I think we can understand what he means.

18 *For affliction does not come from the dust, / nor does trouble sprout from the ground; / but man is born to trouble / as the sparks fly upward.* (Jb 5:6-7)

Trouble is an essential and inevitable thing in this stage of our existence. We are "born" to it. Our day-to-day life is full of it. It is part of our universal environment. No one escapes it. Commonsense would tell us, therefore, that there must be something bound up in trouble which is necessary for us, something without which we should suffer a grievous loss.

It cannot be, as so many seem to think, because of neglect on God's part that trouble should be so universal, for the Bible plainly teaches that it is a part of our birthright. "Man that is born of woman," we are told, "is of few days and full of trouble"; and the psalmist, in considering this, declares that he knows God's judgments to be right and that he has afflicted him in faithfulness.

It is very plain, therefore, that troubles come because of God's faithfulness and not, as so many seem to think, because of his unfaithfulness.

19 *Now Jesus loved Martha and her sister and Lazarus. So when he heard that he was ill, he stayed two days longer in the place where he was. . . . Jesus told them plainly, "Lazarus is dead; and for your sake I am glad that I was not there,*

so that you may believe." . . . Martha said to Jesus, "Lord, if you
had been here, my brother would not have died."

(Jn 11:5-6, 14-15, 21)

He loved them, therefore he stayed away! It was his faithfulness, no this unfaithfulness, that permitted their sorrow to
come upon them without hindrance from him. We may be sure
that what was true of their sorrow is true of our sorrows also. We
say in our ignorance, "If you had been here, this or that would
not have gone wrong"; but if we could see into the heart of the
Lord, we should hear him saying in reply, "I am glad for your
sakes that I was not there." "I am glad." Love can never be glad of
anything that hurts its loved ones, unless there is to come out of
the hurt some infinitely greater blessing. Therefore we may be
sure, no matter how unlikely it may seem, that hidden in every
one of our sorrows is a blessing which it would be a most
grievous loss for us to miss.

20 *For the Lord disciplines him whom he loves, and*
chastises every son whom he receives. (Heb 12:6)

What are the blessings that sorrow and trial bear in their
hands? What is the meaning of the trouble of which the world is
so full?

The answer is to be found in this one sentence, "For the Lord
disciplines him whom he loves, and chastises every son whom
he receives." The meaning of trouble is love. For trouble is not
punishment in our sense of the word; it is chastening. To human
thought the word punishment has a legal sense and means
retribution or vengeance. But God's idea of punishment is the
parental idea of chastening. According to Webster, *chasten*
means "to inflict pain upon any one in order to purify from
errors or faults." God's chastenings, therefore, are for purifying,
not for vengeance. The meaning of trouble, therefore, is plainly
that we may be made "partakers of God's holiness." In other
words, it is for "character building," and character building is to
us the most important thing in the whole universe. What

happens to me is of no account whatever compared to what I am. Therefore, no present ease, or comfort, or absence of trial is to be weighed for a moment against the building up of character for eternity.

21 *He who spares the rod hates his son, / but he who loves him is diligent to discipline him.* (Prv 13:24)

Hate punishes for vengeance, but love punishes for reformation. God has no feelings of vengeance to satisfy toward us, that he sends trouble upon us. But he has a heart of implacable love that cannot be satisfied until it sees us perfect. Let us be thankful, then, that our God loves us enough to chasten us, and let us learn to kiss the rod with which he smites. How thankful we ought to be that our Father in heaven loves us too much to spare the rod and that his love is wise enough to chasten us when we need it!

22 *And I will put this third into the fire, / and refine them as one refines silver, / and test them as gold is tested. / They will call on my name, / and I will answer them. / I will say, "They are my people"; / and they will say, "The Lord is my God."* (Zc 13:9)

To refine anything does not mean to punish it, but only to purify it; to get rid of all its dross and rubbish and to bring out its full beauty and worth. It is a blessing, not a curse. Instead of thinking of it as something God demands of us, it really is something we ought to demand of God. We have a right to be made as pure as God can make us. This is our claim upon him. He created us, and we have a right to demand that he should make out of us the best he can, that he should do this refining work on the creatures he has called into being. It is his duty to burn up our dross and bring out our full beauty and worth. Love demands that he should.

George MacDonald speaks some strong words concerning this: "Man has a claim on God, a divine claim for any pain, want, disappointment, or misery that will help to make him what he ought to be. He has a claim to be punished, and to be spared not one pang that may urge him towards repentance; yea, he has a claim to be compelled to repent; to be hedged in on every side, to have one after another of the strong, sharp-toothed sheep-dogs of the Great Shepherd sent after him, to thwart him in any desire, foil him in any plan, frustrate him of any hope, until he comes to see at length that nothing will ease his pain, nothing make life a thing worth having, but the presence of the living God within him; that nothing is good but the will of God; nothing noble enough for the desire of the heart of man but oneness with the eternal. For this, God must make him yield his very being, that he himself may enter in and dwell with him."

23 *Blessed is the man whom thou dost chasten, O Lord, / and whom thou dost teach out of thy law / to give him respite from days of trouble.* (Ps 94:12-13)

Besides the blessed chastening and refining work of sorrow and trouble, I believe it has often another purpose, and that is to thwart us in a course that our Heavenly Father knows would be disastrous and to turn us into safer and more successful paths. Disappointments are often direct gateways to prosperity in the very things we have thought they were going to ruin for ever. Joseph's story is an illustration of this. He had the promise of a kingdom, but instead he received slavery, and cruel treachery, and imprisonment, and it looked as if all hope of a kingdom was over for ever. But these very trials were the gateway into his kingdom, and in no other way could he have reached it. God's thwartings are often our grandest opportunities.

24 *For the Lord will comfort Zion / he will comfort all her waste places, / and will make her wilderness like Eden, / her desert like the garden of the Lord; / joy and gladness will be found in her, / thanksgiving and the voice of song.* (Is 51:3)

We have often seen our deserts turn into the garden of the

Lord and have found beautiful trees coming up where we thought there were only thorns and briers. The marvelous thing is that we should ever let ourselves become so utterly cast down and overwhelmed when fresh trouble comes. I think it would be a good exercise of soul for us to write out a little record for our own private use of all the times when this marvelous transformation has happened in our experience. It might make us less ready to despair under our next trial.

25 *Will the Lord spurn for ever, / and never again be favorable? / Has his steadfast love for ever ceased? / Are his promises at an end for all time? / Has God forgotten to be gracious? / Has he in anger shut up his compassion?* (Ps 77:7-9)

The natural heart is continually asking such questions as these. Because we cannot see the hand of God in our affairs, we rush to the conclusion that he has lost sight of them and of us. We look at how things seem instead of at the underlying facts. We declare that, because God is unseen, he must necessarily be absent. This is especially true if we are conscious of having ourselves wandered away and forgotten him. We judge him by ourselves and think that he must have also forgotten and forsaken us. We measure his truth by our falseness and find it hard to believe he can be faithful when we know ourselves to be so unfaithful. But there is neither commonsense in this nor divine revelation. How utterly foolish it is, I might even say idiotic, to make our feelings the test of God's actions; as if he came and went in response to the continual changes in our emotions! Such ideas would turn the omnipotent, ever-present God, into a mere helpless puppet, pulled by the strings of our varying emotions! But this, of course, is both inconceivable and impossible; for the God revealed to us in the Bible is a God who never, under any conceivable circumstances, leaves us, or forgets us, or neglects our interests. He is shown to us there as a tender Shepherd, who performs with the utmost fidelity all the shepherd's duties; who does not forsake his sheep in the cloudy and dark day, nor desert them when the wolf comes, but who always draws nearer in every time of need and goes after each sheep that wanders until he finds it. The hireling flees when danger appears because he is a hireling, but the Good Shepherd only sticks closer than ever.

26 *By faith he [Moses] left Egypt, not being afraid of the anger of the king; for he endured as seeing him who is invisible.* (Heb 11:27)

This is the vital point, to see "him who is invisible." Everything hinges on this; and the difference between a triumphant Christian and a despondent one generally arises from the fact that the former has his eyes opened to the hidden God in all things, while the latter is full of doubts as to his presence. But since he has himself said, "I will never leave you nor forsake you," surely every one of us is bound to believe him and to assert boldly, in spite of every appearance to the contrary, our unwavering confidence in the fact of his abiding presence and his unfailing care.

27 *For Israel hath not been forsaken, nor Judah of his God, of the Lord of hosts; though their land was filled with sin against the Holy One of Israel.* (Jer 51:5, KJV)

Even though their land was "filled with sin against the Holy One of Israel," still God did not forsake them. Through all the time of Israel's backsliding, although often unable to manifest himself because of their hardness of heart, still he was with them, their hidden caretaker and protector. The Book of Esther is a striking example of this. The name Esther means secret or hidden, and the whole book is a story of the hidden presence of God in the midst of his people, at a time when their backsliding had so blinded their eyes that they could not see him. Not once in the whole book is the name of God mentioned. Yet his overruling care and guidance were never more manifest than in the events here recorded. The children of Israel seemed to have forgotten God, and to have left him out of all their thoughts; and to them, no doubt, it must have seemed as if he had likewise forgotten them. But behind all their neglect of him and his apparent forgetfulness of them, he held the reins of his providence, and by a series of apparently natural events, and by most unlikely means, using a drunken king, a deceiving woman, a sleepless night, an upstart servant, and a malicious enemy as links in the chain, he brought to pass his will concerning them, and saved them in the time of their need. He does the same now for his people, watching over them the most tenderly at the very moments when he seems the most hidden. This is the case even when the hiding has been caused by our own unfaithfulness or backsliding. We may forsake him, but he never forsakes us, no matter how much it may seem as if he has.

28 *Why do you say, O Jacob, / and speak, O Israel, / "My way is hid from the Lord, / and my right is disregarded by my God"? / Have you not known? Have you not heard? / The Lord is the everlasting God, / the Creator of the ends of the earth.*
(Is 40:27-28)

When we say with Jacob, "My way is hid from the Lord," it is because we do not know God. He is hidden from us, and we think he is therefore absent; we do not see him and we think he does not see us. Like a child in delirium that cannot see its mother, although she is holding it tenderly in her arms, and that calls out in despair, "O mother, mother, come!" so we in the delirium of our unbelief call out, "How long will you forget me, O Lord? For ever? How long will you hide your face from me?" All the time his arms are underneath us, and his love surrounds us on every side.

29 *When the servant of the man of God rose early in the morning and went out, behold, an army with horses and chariots was round about the city. And the servant said, "Alas, my master! What shall we do?" He said, "Fear not, for those who are with us are more than those who are with them."*
(2 Kgs 6:15-16)

God may be hidden from us, but we can never be hidden from him. This scene in the life of Elisha illustrates this. The king of Syria was warring against Israel, but his designs were continually frustrated by Elisha. At last he determined to take Elisha captive, and sent an army to surround the prophet's city. When Elisha's servant saw the forces arrayed against his master, he was dismayed. But Elisha prayed that the Lord would open the eyes of his servant. "So the Lord opened the eyes of the young man, and he saw; and behold, the mountain was full of horses and chariots of fire round about Elisha." Were our eyes but opened, as were the eyes of the servant, we too should see in every time of trial or danger, the mountains round about us full of the horses and chariots of God!

30 *That very day two of them were going to a village named Emmaus, about seven miles from Jerusalem, and talking with each other about all these things that had happened. While they were talking and discussing together, Jesus himself drew near and went with them. But their eyes were kept from recognizing him.* (Lk 24:13-16)

Now as then it often happens that the Lord is walking with his people, as he did with the two disciples on their way to Emmaus. But, like them, we do not know him. We need to have our eyes opened that we may see him. These disciples saw with their bodily eyes, but we are to see with our spiritual eyes. Our seeing is to be by believing. Faith is the soul's eyesight. The word *see* is used not only of the sense of vision by which we perceive external objects, but also of that inward perception which gives us a certain knowledge of spiritual things. We say, for instance, of a mathematical problem, "I see it," meaning, not that our outward eyes see it worked out on a blackboard, but that our inward perception grasps it as an ascertained fact. It is in this sense that we shall come to see him who is invisible, not with our outward eyes, but with the inward eye of our deepest perceptions. In other words, if we would discover the hidden God, we must simply believe, in spite of every appearance to the contrary, that he is with us and is watching over us and caring for us every minute of the day. Though we see him not, we must believe he is there, and, so believing, we shall surely "rejoice with joy unspeakable and full of glory!"

31 *They that strive for the mastery are temperate in all things.* (1 Cor 9:25, KJV)

The law of temperance prescribes only *moderation*, but for many people the only possible way to moderation is by the vigorous practice of abstinence. However strange it may seem, it is found to be easier for many to abstain altogether than to permit a moderate indulgence. Therefore there is nothing to boast of in total abstinence. But for the sake of oneself, and also for the sake of others, the way of safety lies there. To be truly temperate and fully to meet the requirements of health of body, gives an ample field for will-training—a more ample field, it is to be feared, than most of us are cultivating. Few things, however, are a more severe test or a better training of the willpower of a man than fidelity to this trust of the body.

June

1

We are treated ... as having nothing, and yet possessing everything. (2 Cor 6:8, 10)

The Apostle Paul gives us this paradox as one of the foundation principles of the Christian life: having nothing and yet possessing everything. It is a saying of the deepest significance, for it strikes a blow at the whole fabric of the ordinary Christian life. The ambition of most Christians is to have a vast number of things; and their energies are all wasted in the vain effort to get possession of these things. Some strive to possess certain "experiences"; some seek after "ecstatic feelings"; some try to make themselves rich in theological "views" and "dogmas"; some store up a long list of works done and results achieved; some seek to acquire "illuminations" or to accumulate "gifts" and "graces." In short, all Christians, almost without exception, seek to possess a store of something or other, which they fancy will serve to recommend them to God and make them worthy of his love and care. Could we but understand clearly the meaning of Paul's words: "having nothing, and yet possessing everything," all this would be at an end. For we would see that the one thing God wants of us is that we should empty ourselves of all our own things, in order that we may be brought to depend on him for everything; we should discover that his purpose is to bring us to the place where we have nothing apart from himself.

2 *But to the tribe of Levi Moses gave no inheritance; the Lord God of Israel is their inheritance, as he said to them.* (Jos 13:33)

"I am thine inheritance." What an amazing saying! No wonder the Levites were content to go without any other possessions! Having nothing, they truly possessed all things, for God was their possession! How slow we are to see that this is our privilege now, just as truly as it was that of the Levites in those days of old. Apart from Christ we, in fact, have nothing, for moth and rust are sure to corrupt, and thieves to break through and steal all merely human possessions. But if God is ours, then all things are eternally ours, for what belongs to God must of necessity belong to us also according to our need and our measure.

3 *Blessed be the God and Father of our Lord Jesus Christ, who has blessed us in Christ with every spiritual blessing in the heavenly places.* (Eph 1:3)

It is here declared that all things have been given to us freely in Christ, but as a matter of fact we may not yet ourselves have taken possession of them all. When our hands are full of our own things, we cannot possibly take possession of the things of God. Only empty hands can grasp a gift; only empty vessels can receive the filling; and only the heart that is emptied of all its own things can receive the things of God. I mean, for instance, that if Christians are enjoying very ecstatic "experiences," they cannot help resting in them and will feel no need to find their rest in God alone. Therefore it is that God finds it so often necessary to take away all our own things and to leave us empty and bereft of all that we have most valued. He dries up our "fervors"; he deadens our "feelings"; he spoils our "experiences";

he confuses our "views"; he clouds our "illuminations"; and so brings us at last to the place where, having nothing of our own, we are driven to find our rest in the things of God. I believe this is the explanation of the dark and perplexing times through which many of God's children are called to pass, when they seem to have lost all the joy and clearness of their earlier experiences and to have been plunged into a fog of darkness and distress. Did they but understand it, they would give God thanks that, in his tender love, he is thus depriving them of all their own possessions; since it is only so that he can bring them safely and surely to the place where they will be content to possess him alone. "Having nothing," they will at last "possess all things."

4 *Let him who glories glory in this, that he understands and knows me, that I am the Lord who practice steadfast love, justice and righteousness in the earth; for in these things I delight, says the Lord. (Jer 9:24)*

Have any of us ever come to the place where we have honestly ceased to glory in our own possessions? Never, I believe, until we have been deprived of them. Human nature is so constituted that while it possesses anything, it can hardly help glorying in it. As long as a Christian feels wise or strong or rich in spiritual things, that Christian will almost inevitably glory in his strength, wisdom, or riches. But if these are taken away, he will be driven to glory in the Lord alone, simply because there will be nothing else to glory in.

5 *Do not labor for the food which perishes, but for the food which endures to eternal life, which the Son of man will give to you; for on him has God the Father set his seal. (Jn 6:27)*

Everything that perishes belongs to the sphere of earthly things. Experiences perish; feelings perish; views perish; doctrines perish; the Apostle tells us that prophecies fail, and tongues cease, and knowledge vanishes away. It is impossible, therefore, that any of these perishable things, no matter how good they may be, could really satisfy the imperishable spirit. But while we labor for and hold on to the perishable things, we shall have no energy to seek after the "food which endures to eternal life."

I do not mean by this that the soul should not have any experiences, no views, doctrines, knowledge, or strength. Paul had all these in greater measure, I suppose, than anyone else ever had, and yet he could declare that he had "nothing." What he meant was that he had nothing apart from Christ, but that he had all things in Christ. That is, Christ was his strength and wisdom and righteousness, and in himself he had nothing. I know this is a little difficult to explain. The illustration that helps me the most, though an imperfect one, is that of steam working through an engine. The engine has no power of its own, but all its power is derived from the steam that works through it. Could the machinery speak, its language would be similar to Paul's, "having nothing, and yet possessing all things."

6 *He is the source of your life in Christ Jesus, whom God made our wisdom, our righteousness and sanctification and redemption.* (1 Cor 1:30)

We must set aside our own wisdom and righteousness in order that Christ may be made wisdom and righteousness and sanctification for us. Practically, this means, that if I want righteousness of any kind I must not try to lay up a store of it within myself, but must draw my supplies of righteousness, moment by moment, from the Lord. I remember once feeling the need of a great stock of patience to meet an emergency that was coming upon me. I thought I would be obliged to pray for a long time in order to lay up enough. I think I expected something like a package of patience, done up and labeled "Patience," and deposited in my heart. As I was preparing myself to pray all night long in order to lay in a good supply, suddenly this verse flashed into my mind: *whom God made our wisdom, our righteousness and sanctification and redemption.* "Yes," I added with a sudden illumination, "and patience too! I do not need to lay up a stock of patience; all the patience I need is stored up for me in Christ, and I have only to draw my supplies momentarily from him." I rose from my knees at once and thanked the Lord beforehand for the unlimited supply of patience that I saw was mine in Christ. I need not say that I found grace (in the form of patience) to help in every time of need.

7   *Whatever gain I had, I counted as loss for the sake of Christ.... For his sake I have suffered the loss of all things, and count them as refuse, in order that I may gain Christ and be found in him.* (Phil 3:7-8)

The loss of all things meant to Paul the gain of all things. The loss of the nest to the young eaglet, who is just learning to fly, means the gain of the whole heavens for its home. The loss of our own strength means the gaining of God's strength in its place; the loss of our own wisdom means the gaining of God's wisdom; the loss of our own life means the gaining of God's life. Who would not make the exchange?

8   *One man pretends to be rich, yet has nothing; / another pretends to be poor, yet has great wealth.* (Prv 13:7)

To which of these two classes do we belong? Are we seeking to make ourselves rich, or are we content to be poor and possess nothing? I used to have a friend who talked a great deal about what she called the "stripping chamber." She was one of those who are continually trying to "make themselves rich" by seeking after "experiences" and "blessings," and she could not seem to understand why the Lord found it necessary so continually to strip her of all that she had gained. A little book called *The Saint's Travel to the Land of Canaan* thus describes this stripping process: "God in these days is discovering the false coverings of creatures, and so stripping them naked. He is bringing men to see the great mystery of self in all its supposed glory. He is annihilating creatures, and bringing them to a spiritual death. He is laying low mountains, and is unbottoming creatures from their false rests. Men's lofty looks He is abasing; yea, He is bringing men, who have been as it were Stars, and of great account in their own and in others' eyes, even to a loss and silence, confusion and darkness; so that now their light seems to be darkness, their wisdom folly, their life death; and their enlargements and self-actings are hedged up, and they cannot find out any of their former paths. And all this is that the creature may be brought to depend on the Creator, and have nothing apart from Him."

9 *Every one who has left houses or brothers or sisters or father or mother or children or lands, for my name's sake, will receive a hundredfold, and inherit eternal life.* (Mt 19:29)

All that we have, whether outward or inward, must be left behind if we would receive the hundredfold of God. It must be left behind, not in the sense of literally getting rid of everything, but in the sense of having everything only in and from the Lord. The real facts of the case are that only God knows how to take care of things as they ought to be taken care of, and he alone is able to do it; therefore nothing is really safe until it is handed over to his care. The most unsafe person in the universe to have charge of my things is myself; and never do I possess them so firmly as when I have transferred them into the hands of God and have left them in his charge. Never am I so sure of my money as when I have transferred it out of my unsafe pockets into the safe custody of a trustworthy bank; and the same thing is true regarding the abandonment of all I possess into the custody of God. It may be considered a very pious thing to do, but it is certainly only good commonsense as well.

10 *If with Christ you died to the elemental spirits of the universe, why do you live as if you still belonged to the world? Why do you submit to regulations, . . . according to* *human precepts and doctrines? These have indeed an appearance of wisdom . . . but they are of no value in checking the indulgence of the flesh.* (Col 2:20-23)

Our feelings, our experiences, our exercises of various sorts often have the "appearance of wisdom," and it is hard for us to count them as really nothing and to say truly, when we seem to have so many things, that we have nothing. But anything that is wrought out by "flesh" in any way whatever, must always be "nothing" in the sight of God; and, as soon as we have learned to see things with his eyes, they will be nothing in our own sight also. The simple fact is that all our own possessions of any kind whatsoever are literally and truly "nothing." No matter how many we may have of them, we still must say with the Apostle, if we speak the truth, that we "have nothing."

11 *Every devoted thing is most holy to the Lord.* (Lv 27:28)

Everything that is set apart for God becomes holy. His possession of it is what makes it holy, whatever it may have been before. This is a blessed truth to the poor soul that feels its unholiness and yet longs to be only the Lord's.

Satan continually tempts such to think that they are too unholy for the Lord to accept, and what he suggests about their unworthiness is so true that it seems impossible to argue with his conclusions. But the answer here is simply this, that the altar sanctifies the gift, that anything given to the Lord is made holy by the very fact of being so given. Even our bodies, if presented to him as a living sacrifice, are thereby rendered "holy and acceptable."

Just as we have sometimes read in our childish tales of a water that changed everything put into it into gold, so here we read of a God so infinite in holiness that everything devoted to him becomes holy by his simple possession of it. Take comfort then, dear humble soul, and transfer at once yourself and all that you have into this grand possession, that it may all become "most holy to the Lord."

12 For what person knows a man's thoughts except the spirit of the man which is in him? So also no one comprehends the thoughts of God except the Spirit of God.

(1 Cor 2:11)

The one essential for each of us is to have this spiritual man, this resurrection life, born in us. Nothing avails but this. The tiger cannot understand the thoughts of a man because it does not have the spirit of a man within it. Likewise, we cannot understand the thoughts of God unless we possess the spirit of God.

The new birth is a necessity in the very nature of things, for in order to enter any plane of life we must be born into it. No amount of effort can turn a tiger into a man, and no amount of effort can turn the flesh man into the spirit man. That which is born of the flesh *is* flesh and always must be.

13 And the effect of righteousness will be peace, / and the result of righteousness, quietness and trust for ever. / My people will abide in a peaceful habitation, / in secure dwellings, and in quiet resting places. (Is 32:17-18)

There may be storms outside; but within, the "habitation" of the spirit is a "quiet resting place" in God. To sit still or to wait, therefore, does not interfere with outward activity, but is, in fact, the source of its strength. If I am working at anything outwardly and am inwardly at rest about it, I shall do it far more successfully than if I fret and fume and fuss inwardly. This is a matter of universal commonsense experience.

14 And behold, the Lord passed by, and a great and strong wind rent the mountains, and broke in pieces the rocks before the Lord, but the Lord was not in the wind; and after the wind an earthquake; and after the earthquake a fire, but the Lord was not in the fire; and after the fire a still small voice.

(1 Kgs 19:11-12)

Only in the silence can the "still small voice" be heard. A large part of the difficulty experienced by Christians in hearing the voice of the Lord arises from the absence of this inward stillness. Our own internal clamor drowns his quiet speaking. We listen for his voice "in the wind" and "in the earthquake," expecting their thunder to sound above all our own clamoring; and because we are disappointed, we complain that he does not speak at all; when all the while, the "still small voice" of his love is waiting for the quiet in which it can be heard. I am convinced that there are many at this moment hungering for the voice of the Lord, who would hear it at once if they would only be silent before him for a little while. All the saints of old have insisted upon stillness as a necessity of true communion with God and have exhorted their followers to cultivate it; and every saint of the present day knows its value.

15 *The word of the Lord came to me, saying, "You have shed much blood and have waged great wars; you shall not build a house to my name, because you have shed so much blood before me upon the earth. Behold, a son shall be born to you; he shall be a man of peace. . . . He shall build a house for my name." (1 Chr 22:8-10)*

To know the indwelling of the Lord as a conscious experience, there must be inward quiet. Where there are wars and fightings inwardly, his presence cannot be realized. I do not mean that when the soul is in conflict the Lord has forsaken it. A thousand times, No! The Lord was with David just as truly as he was with Solomon; but it required a "man of peace" to build the house to his name, and not a man in the midst of wars. What I mean is only this, that his indwelling presence cannot be consciously realized when we are in the midst of internal wars; and that to have the conscious experience of his indwelling, we must be at rest inwardly and must know what it is to "keep silence" from all our fears and anxieties and all our fussings and worryings.

16 *But we beseech you, brethren, that you increase more and more; and that you study to be quiet, and to do your own business, and to work with your own hands, as we commanded you.* (1 Thes 4:10-11, KJV)

"Study to be quiet," that is, study to dismiss all bustle and worry out of your inward life. Study also to "do your own business," and do not try to do the business of other people. A great deal of "creaturely activity" is expended in trying to do other people's business. It is often very hard to sit still when we see our friends mismanaging matters and making what we think to be such dreadful blunders. But the divine order is for each one of us to do our own business and to refrain from meddling with the business of anyone else.

17 *"Be still, and know that I am God. / I am exalted among the nations, / I am exalted in the earth!" / The Lord of hosts is with us; / the God of Jacob is our refuge.* (Ps 46:10-11)

In order to really know God, this inward stillness is absolutely necessary. I remember when I first learned this. A time of great emergency had arisen in my life, when every part of my being seemed to throb with anxiety, and when the necessity for immediate and vigorous action seemed overpowering. Yet circumstances were such that I could do nothing. For a little while it seemed as if I would fly to pieces with the inward turmoil. Suddenly the still, small voice whispered in the depths of my soul, "Be still, and know that I am God." The word came with power, and I listened. I composed my body to perfect stillness, and I constrained my troubled spirit into quietness and looked up and waited. And then did I "know" that it was God, God even in the very emergency, and in my very helplessness to meet it; and I rested in him. He was exalted "among the nations" and in my "earth." It was an experience that I would not have missed for anything. Out of this stillness seemed to arise a power to deal with the emergency that very soon brought it to a successful conclusion.

18 *Jesus immediately reached out his hand and caught him, saying to him, "O man of little faith, why did you doubt?"* (Mt 14:31)

"Why did you doubt?" This is a most significant question. It is as though our Lord had said, "Knowing me as you do, Peter, and having experienced all my love and care for you for so long, how is it that you can doubt me now? If I have called you to come to me on the water, of course I will enable you to do so. What are boisterous winds or tossing waves to me, the Creator and Ruler of them all? Why do you doubt?"

This question is as full of significance now as it was on that stormy night in Galilee, almost 2,000 years ago. It might well be asked of thousands of Christians living on the earth at the present moment. For when winds are contrary and seas are stormy with us, doubts and fears are as near at hand to overwhelm us as they were near at hand to Peter; and the reproach, "O man of little faith," applies as definitely to many of Christ's disciples now as it did to Peter then.

19 *And he awoke and rebuked the wind, and said to the sea, "Peace! Be still!" And the wind ceased, and there was a great calm. He said to them, "Why are you afraid? Have you no faith?"* (Mk 4:39-40)

The disciples of Jesus became frightened when a storm arose at sea. Their fright was not caused by the great storm to which they were exposed, but by their own lack of faith. Storms cannot frighten people who are trusting in the Lord. Doubt is the origin of every fear that can possibly assail the child of God.

"He who listens to me will dwell secure / and will be at ease, without dread of evil." Most people do not listen to God, but instead to their own fears. The soul that really listens to the Lord knows there is absolutely nothing to be afraid of and will declare triumphantly with the psalmist, "The Lord is my light and my salvation; whom shall I fear? The Lord is the strength of my life; of whom shall I be afraid?" And it will answer its own questions with the confident assertion, "Though a host should encamp against me, my heart shall not fear!" Not all the hosts of earth or hell can frighten the soul that "listens to God."

20 *He said, "Come." So Peter got out of the boat and walked on the water and came to Jesus; but when he saw the wind, he was afraid and beginning to sink he cried out, "Lord, save me." (Mt 14:29-30)*

How reasonable and sensible our doubts seem. "Look, Peter," the tempter most probably said, "look at those roaring waves, and remember that such a thing was never heard of—that a man could walk on water. It is really presumptuous for you to try to do so. The Master does not mean for you actually to go to him. It is only a figure of speech; and if you do not want to be drowned, you had better get back to a safe place on the ship as fast as you can." It is amazing to me, however, that Peter could listen for a moment to these suggestions of doubt when he had heard the Master's command. Yet in the face of hundreds of similar commands and promises, Christians now listen to far worse suggestions of doubt and even think they are pious and humble in doing so! It is simply amazing!

21 *Fear not, for I am with you, / be not dismayed for I am your God; / I will strengthen you, I will help you, / I will uphold you with my victorious right hand. (Is 41:10-14)*

The Bible is full of these "fear nots," with their accompanying assurances that God will be with us and will certainly care for us. If we believe these assurances, no enemies and no dangers, whether they are outward or inward, can cause us a moment's fear or doubt; for we will know that the Lord our God is stronger than any enemy the universe contains, and we will say with the Apostle, "If God is for me, who can be against me?"

22 *For God did not give us a spirit of timidity but a spirit of power and love and self-control. (2 Tm 1:7)*

The "spirit of timidity," or fear, does not belong to the Christian religion. It is never enumerated among the "fruits of the Spirit." It is not given to us from God. On the contrary, it is always condemned as being alien to the whole idea of Christianity and as coming purely and only from unbelief.

23 *He who conquers shall have this heritage, and I will be his God and he shall be my son. But as for the cowardly, the faithless, the polluted, as for murderers, fornicators, sorcerers, idolaters, and all liars, their lot shall be in the lake that burns with fire and sulphur, which is the second death.*

(Rv 21:7-8)

It is a most significant fact that among the sins which are here declared to plunge a soul into the lake of fire that of being "cowardly and faithless" heads the list. All that this means I do not know, but I am certain it must mean this much, that to be fearful and faithless, or unbelieving, is as absolute a hindrance to the spiritual life as many things which we consider far greater sins. This leaves us no alternative as to whether or not we shall go on indulging in the habit of doubt. We dare not do it. We must get rid of our doubts somehow. The only question is how? To this I would reply that there is only one way. We must *give them up.* We must surrender them to the Lord and must trust him to deliver us from their power. Doubts are a "speaking against God" and are consequently sin. They are not an infliction, but a rebellion. We can never indulge in them for a single moment without disobeying our Lord, who has left us, as his last command, this law: "Let not your heart be troubled, neither let it be afraid." No matter how plausible our doubts may seem, we simply must turn our backs on them and refuse to entertain them for a moment.

You must hand your doubting over to him, as you do your temper or your pride, and must trust him to deliver you from doubting, just as you do to deliver you from getting angry. The great point is to give up the liberty to doubt. No surrender is really effective until it reaches the point of saying "I will not." Therefore our only hope for victory lies in an utter surrender of all liberty to doubt.

24 *Blessed is the man who endures temptation: for when he has been proved, he will receive the crown of life which the Lord has promised to those who love him.*

(Jas 1:12, NKJV)

The first thing that I would say concerning temptation is that temptation is not sin. The second thing I would say is the same, and the third thing is the same also. It may seem to some as if this hardly needed to be said so emphatically, because everyone must already know it; but I believe, on the contrary, that very few really know it. Our text tells us that it is a blessed thing to endure temptation; but do we really believe it to be a blessed thing? Do we not usually feel, instead, that it is a cursed thing; and that we must be dreadful sinners just because we are tempted? A flood of evil thoughts is poured into our souls, proud thoughts, unkind thoughts, malicious thoughts, jealous thoughts. They are thoughts we loathe, and yet they seem to come from inside us; and we feel that we must be very wicked and very far from God to be able to have such thoughts at all. It is as though a burglar should break into a man's house. When the master of the house tries to resist him and drive him out, the burglar turns around and accuses the owner of being himself the thief! It is the enemy's grand ruse for entrapping us. He whispers his suggestions of evil into our hearts and then turns around and says, "Oh, how wicked you must be to think of such things! It is very plain you cannot be a child of God; for if you were, it would have been impossible for such dreadful thoughts to have entered your heart." This reasoning sounds so very plausible, that the Christian feels as if it must be true and is plunged into the depths of discouragement and despair. But the divine teaching about temptation is very different.

25 *In this you rejoice, though now for a little while you may have to suffer various trials, so that the genuineness of your faith, more precious than gold which though perishable is tested by fire, may redound to praise and glory and honor at the revelation of Jesus Christ.* (1 Pt 1:6-7)

Temptations try our faith; and we are worth nothing if we are not tried. They develop our spiritual virtues, and this development is essential to our true growth. How shallow would be our spirituality if it were not for the discipline of temptation! There is, therefore, in the divine plan evidently a need for such trials during the "little while" of our earthly life. The "genuineness of our faith" is so much more precious to the Lord and so much more valuable for us than any present comfort or ease, that he is willing to let us suffer these trials. This was his way with the children of Israel. When God took them into the promised land, he did not drive out at once all their enemies, but left some to "prove them," that he might know whether or not they would listen to his commandments (see Jgs 2:21-23; and 3:1-4).

I have sometimes thought that temptation is to our soul's health what vaccination is to our body's health, a process by which we are prepared for the victory over far worse attacks of far worse diseases.

26 *Because he himself has suffered and been tempted, he is able to help those who are tempted.* (Heb 2:18)

If we believe that our Lord was really tempted, just as we are, we cannot help but be convinced that temptation is not sin, and that it is possible to have temptations of every kind, and yet be "without sin." We may be sure of this, also, that wherever temptation is, there is the Lord, waiting to help us. "Where were you, Lord, while I was being tempted?" cried the saint in the desert. "Close beside you all the while, my son, giving you the needed grace to conquer your temptation," was the tender reply.

27 *No temptation has overtaken you that is not common to man. God is faithful, and he will not let you be tempted beyond your strength, but with the temptation will also provide the way of escape, that you may be able to endure it.*
(1 Cor 10:13)

Fenelon says concerning temptation: "We must never be astonished at temptations, be they ever so outrageous. On this earth all is temptation. Crosses tempt us by irritating our pride, and prosperity by flattering it. Our life is a continual combat, but one in which Jesus Christ fights for us. While temptations rage around us, we must pass on unmoved, as the traveler overtaken by a storm simply wraps his cloak more closely about him, and pushes on more vigorously towards his destined home."

28 *Hear, O Israel, you draw near this day to battle against your enemies: let not your heart faint; do not fear, or tremble, or be in dread of them; for the Lord your God is he that goes with you, to fight for you against your enemies, to give you the victory.* (Dt 20:3-4)

"The Lord your God is he that goes with you, to fight for you against your enemies." This is the whole secret. I once asked a Christian, whose life of victory over temptation had greatly impressed me, what his secret was. He replied that it all lay in this, that the Lord fought for him and he held his peace. "Once," he said, "I used to feel that I had to do the fighting myself; and it always seemed to me that the Lord was behind me to help me if the emergency became too great, but that for the most part he looked on and left the fighting to me. But now," he continued, "I put the Lord in front, and he does the fighting, while I look on and behold the victory."

29 *Stand therefore, having girded your loins with truth, and having put on the breastplate of righteousness, and having shod your feet with the equipment of the gospel of peace;*

besides all these taking the shield of faith, with which you can quench all the flaming darts of the evil one. And take the helmet of salvation, and the sword of the Spirit, which is the word of God. (Eph 6:14-17)

All this is the armor of faith. Our Lord used this armor in his conflict with temptation in the wilderness (see Lk 4:1-13). This story gives us a vivid insight into the reality of the declaration that he was "in all points" tempted as we are. His example shows us how we are to conquer. The weapon he used was the "sword of the Spirit," which is, the Apostle tells us, the "word of God." He met each temptation with some saying from the Bible, introducing each by the words "It is written." I believe that the truth as it is revealed in scripture is always our most effective weapon against temptation. I say weapon, because I do not mean that it is our power. The power to conquer comes from the Lord alone, but the weapons are put into our hands; and, to my mind, chief among these is the one used by Christ, i.e., the word, or truth, of God. I believe that there is nearly always some "It is written" with which we can meet and conquer every form of temptation.

30 *Ye are they which have continued with me in my temptations. And I appoint unto you a kingdom, as my Father hath appointed unto me; that ye may eat and drink at my table in my kingdom, and sit on thrones judging the twelve tribes of Israel. (Lk 22:28-30, KJV).*

One great mistake we make about temptations is to feel as if the time spent in enduring them was all lost time. Days pass, perhaps, and we have been so beset with temptations that we feel that we have made no progress. But it often happens that we have been serving the Lord far more truly while "continuing with him" in temptation, than we could have done in our times of comparative freedom from it. Temptation is as much an attack against God as against ourselves, and we are fighting his battles quite as much as our own when we resist it. Moreover the "kingdom" which has been "appointed" to us can only come through this pathway of manifold temptations.

July

1 *I have loved you with an everlasting love;/ therefore I have continued my faithfulness to you. (Jer 31:3)*

Another law of divine love is that it is everlasting. It has had no beginning and can have no end. So little is this understood that many people have a rooted conviction that God only begins to love them after they have shown him that they love him; and that he ceases to love them the moment they in any way displease him. They look upon his love as a fickle sort of thing, not in the least to be depended upon, and are always questioning whether they may reckon it to be theirs or not.

2 *A new commandment I give to you, that you love one another; even as I have loved you, that you also love one another. By this all men will know that you are my disciples, if you have love for one another. (Jn 13:34-35)*

We all have an ideal about what love between human beings ought to be, and we experience a sense of condemnation whenever we fail to come up to our standard. Now if it is true that we are to love one another as Christ loves us, the converse

113

must also be true, that Christ must love us as we know we ought to love one another. In other words, the law of love from God to us is exactly the same as the law of love from us to one another; and what love demands from me to my brother or sister is what love demands from God to me. This is a far more important point than might appear at first. I am convinced that wrong views of the love of God lie at the root of most of our spiritual difficulties. We take the worst elements in our own characters—our selfishness, our impatience, our suspicion, our hard thoughts of one another—as the key to interpret God, instead of taking our best elements—our love, self-sacrifice, and patience, as the key. And so we subvert every single law of love in our interpretation of God, who is love itself.

3 *Love bears all things, believes all things, hopes all things, endures all things.* (1 Cor 13:7)

Still another law of love is that it is not easily provoked and that it thinks no evil, but bears all things and hopes all things. Mothers understand this law and are always thinking the best of their children, believing and hoping, and enduring until the end of their lives. If the child is naughty, they say, "Poor darling, she is sick"; or, "Poor boy, we must remember his temptations." But these same mothers, perhaps, will think of God as if he were always looking out with an unfriendly eye for the least imperfection in themselves, and were even putting the worst possible construction upon their motives, thinking evil of them even when they really meant well.

4 *Love your enemies and pray for those who persecute you, so that you may be sons of your Father who is in heaven. . . . You, therefore, must be perfect, as your heavenly Father is perfect.* (Mt 5:44-45, 48)

The perfection here spoken of is the perfection of love. In order to be children of our Father in the only true sense of this expression, namely, oneness of nature and character, we must love our enemies, for he loves his enemies. This exhortation of our Lord's would of course lose all its point if God did not love his enemies. No more tremendous assertion of God's universal love to all mankind, even to those who are his enemies, is made throughout the whole Bible than is incidentally contained in this passage. I am to love my enemies because God loves his. If he does not love his enemies, then I need not love mine. It is as clear as daylight. But this is only incidental. The point of the passage is, that if I would be perfect in my measure, as God is in his, I must love. Love is the sign-manual and the test.

5 What shall we say, then? That Gentiles who did not pursue righteousness have attained it, that is, righteousness through faith; but that Israel who pursued the righteousness which is based on law did not succeed in fulfilling that law.
(Rom 9:30-31)

Everyone realizes that righteousness is absolutely vital to the spiritual life, not only on Sundays, but on each day of the week as well. But, like the Israelites of whom our text speaks, how many there are who do not attain to it and whose souls cry out in bitter questioning, "Why?"

Let the scriptures answer their cry. "Because they did not pursue it through faith, but as if it were based on works." No answer could be clearer than this. Faith is the law of spiritual righteousness, and righteousness is to be attained in no other way. No amount of works, however religious, can bring about true holiness. Outward actions can never take the soul into the inner sanctuary of the righteousness of God. The reason for this is evident. God's righteousness is a righteousness of nature or being, and outward actions can never create inward life; they can only reveal it. God is not righteous because he does righteous deeds, but he does righteous deeds because he is righteous. This is the essential difference between the righteousness of faith and the righteousness of works. The last is a righteousness put on from the outside; the first springs up from within. The one is works; the other is fruit.

6 You hypocrites! Well did Isaiah prophesy of you, when he said: "This people honors me with their lips, / but their heart is far from me; / in vain do they worship me, / teaching as doctrines the precepts of men." (Mt 15:7-9)

It is all "in vain" for us to think that any righteousness which is only outside can be acceptable to God or of any worth to ourselves. Nothing was more universally condemned by our Lord, and nothing was more despised by the Apostles. If ever any man had reason to glory in his outward righteousness, it was Paul. He had been zealous and faithful in all that his religion demanded of him, and could even say of himself that "touching the righteousness that is in the law" he had been blameless; and yet, in the face of the reality of true inward righteousness in Christ, he counted all this outward righteousness to be but dung, that he might "win Christ and be found in him, not having his own righteousness, which is of the law, but that which is through the faith of Christ, the righteousness which is of God by faith" (see Phil 3:4-9).

Paul had learned that only the "righteousness which is of God by faith" could satisfy the longings of his awakened spiritual nature. Every child of God must learn the same lesson. Our souls cry out for something that is real. We go through all the faithful rounds of outward activities; we give up this; we consent to that; we perform every known duty; we are obedient to all requirements; and yet we are not satisfied. We feel, as our Lord himself has said, that the righteousness that belongs to the kingdom of God must "exceed" this outward righteousness, just as the inward reality always exceeds the outward show; and we cannot be satisfied short of it.

7 For Christ is the end of the law, that every one who has faith may be justified. (Rom 10:4)

Christ is the end of all our self-efforts after righteousness, not "at the end," as I used to think, but the actual ending of them. For he is our righteousness. That is, the life of Christ in our souls is a righteous life, which produces all right outward actions by the power of its inward workings. Therefore, in the very nature of things, it puts an end to any need for establishing our own righteousness. Instead of our efforts to take possession of righteousness, the life of Christ in our souls makes righteousness take possession of us. We are controlled from within and not from without.

8 *She seeks wool and flax, / and works with willing hands.*
(Prv 31:13)

When men and women first began to toil, not their fall, but their salvation, was begun.

When a man cleared his first field of thistles, and in his work his sweat fell heavy on the rescued soil, his joy and not his sorrow began; for labor ends in delight, and is the only mother of true rest; and it is by what a thing ends in, and not by what it is while it is being done, that we judge the thing. Out of the noble pains of labor, struggling with all the reluctant elements of nature, have streamed into humanity all the blessings it has loved and rejoiced in—all knowledge, all discovery, the interests which awake and kindle us, poetry and art, law, civil order, the gentleness and greatness of life, the high conceptions of the imagination, and all our grasp of nature. Little would we care to go on were it not for the difficulties; little would we care for the results if we had not won them with trouble; little would we care for rest if it were not filled with the exulting memories of our work.

9 *For the Egyptians shall help in vain, and to no purpose: therefore have I cried concerning this, Their strength is to sit still.* (Is 30:7, KJV)

There is immense power in stillness. All of God's greatest creative works are done in silence. All the vital functions of our bodies are silently performed. The moment they make a noise, we are sure they are out of order. If I can hear the beating of my heart, I know at once that something is wrong. If my brain makes a buzzing noise in my ears, I am afraid that something is greatly wrong.

This is far more true of spiritual forces. Their work is always done in the stillness. Faith, that mightiest of all spiritual powers, makes no noise in its inward exercise. The new birth is silently accomplished. The Spirit of God works noiselessly within our hearts and effects all its mighty transformations in deepest stillness. The "creature" in us may accompany all these processes with noise and bustle, but as to the process itself, we must all recognize that it is silently wrought.

10 *"In returning and rest you shall be saved;/ in quietness and in trust shall be your strength." / And you would not, but you said, / "No! We will speed upon horses." (Is 30:15)*

The Israelites of old, like Christians now, could not believe that quietness and rest were the way of strength and deliverance; they tried instead to "speed upon horses," just as we now try to find our deliverance by earthly means and by creaturely activities. It is as useless for us as for them. The truth is, the silent way is the only victorious way. A great student of Christian philosophy once said to me, "All things come to him who knows how to trust and be silent." The words are pregnant with meaning. A knowledge of this fact would immensely change our ways of working. Instead of the restless and wearying struggles of our present methods, we would rest inwardly before the Lord, in "quietness and trust," and would let the divine forces of his spirit work out in silence the ends to which we aspire. You may not see or feel the operations of this silent force, but be assured it is always working mightily and will work for you, if only you can get your spirit still enough to be carried along by the currents of its power.

11 *And Moses said to the people, "Fear not, stand firm, and see the salvation of the Lord, which he will work for you today; for the Egyptians whom you see today, you shall never see again." (Ex 14:13)*

Only when we "stand firm" can we see the salvation of the Lord. Another translation says, "stand still." While full of bustle and hurry, we have no eyes to spare for God's work; our own work absorbs all our interest. Moreover, our creaturely activity, instead of helping, really hinders his working. Spiritual forces cannot have full flow when carnal forces usurp their place. To see God's salvation fully worked out, we must let his power accomplish it all, and must not permit our own "carnal" working to interfere.

12 *When a woman is in travail she has sorrow, because her hour has come; but when she is delivered of the child, she no longer remembers the anguish, for joy that a child is born into the world. So you have sorrow now, but I will see you again and your hearts will rejoice, and no one will take your joy from you.* (Jn 16:21-22)

If we want a "joy that no one can take from us," we must find it in something no one can disturb. No element of joy that is subject to human fluctuations can be in the least depended on. The only lasting joy is to be found in the everlasting God. In God alone, I mean, apart from all else; apart from his gifts, apart from his blessings, apart from all that can by any possibility change or alter. He alone is unchangeable; he is the same good, loving, tender God "yesterday, today, and forever"; and we can rejoice in him always, whether we are able to rejoice in his gifts and his promises or not. We rejoice in a baby just because it is, not because of anything it has done or can do for us; and something like this, only infinitely deeper and wider, does it mean to rejoice in God.

13 *He makes me lie down in green pastures. / He leads me beside still waters; / he restores my soul.* (Ps 23:2)

The role of the sheep is very simple. It is only to trust and to follow. The Shepherd does all the rest. He leads the sheep by the right way. He chooses their paths for them and sees that those paths are paths where the sheep can walk in safety. When he puts forth his sheep, he goes before them. The sheep have none of the planning to do, none of the decisions to make, none of the forethought or wisdom to exercise; they have absolutely nothing to do but to trust themselves entirely to the care of the good Shepherd, and to follow him wherever he leads. It is very simple. There is nothing complicated in trusting when the One we are called upon to trust is absolutely trustworthy, and nothing complicated in obedience when we have perfect confidence in the power we are obeying.

14 *Behold, I am doing a new thing; / now it springs forth, do you not perceive it? / I will make a way in the wilderness and rivers in the desert.* (Is 43:19)

Thousands of the flock of Christ can testify that when they have put themselves absolutely into his hands, he has quieted the raging tempest, and has turned their deserts into blossoming gardens. I do not mean that there will be no more outward trouble or care or suffering; but these very places will become green pastures, and still waters inwardly to the soul. The Shepherd knows what pastures are best for his sheep, and they must not question nor doubt but must trustingly follow him. Perhaps he sees that the best pastures for some of us are to be found in the midst of opposition or of earthly trials. If he leads you there, you may be sure they are green pastures for you, and that you will grow and be made strong by feeding in them.

15 *Call no man your father on earth, for you have one Father, who is in heaven.* (Mt 23:9)

One of the most illuminating names of God is the one especially revealed by our Lord Jesus Christ: the name of Father. I say especially revealed by Christ, because, while God had been called throughout the ages by many other names, expressing other aspects of his character, Christ alone has revealed him to us under the all-inclusive name of Father. This is a name that holds within itself all other names of wisdom and power, and above all of love and goodness, a name that embodies for us a perfect supply for all our needs. Christ, who was the only begotten Son in the bosom of the Father, was the only one who could reveal this name, for he alone knew the Father.

16
I thank thee, Father, Lord of heaven and earth, that thou has hidden these things from the wise and understanding and revealed them to babes. (Lk 10:21)

In the Old Testament, God was revealed as a great warrior fighting for his people, or as a mighty king ruling over them and caring for them. The name of Father is only given to him a very few times there, six or seven at the most; while in the New Testament it is given between two and three hundred times. Christ, who knew him, was the only one who could reveal him. "No man," he said, "knows who the Father is, but the Son, and he to whom the son will reveal him."

The vital question that confronts each of us is whether we individually understand that Christ speaks to us of the Father. We know he uses the word Father continually, but do we in the least understand what the word means? Have we even an inkling of who the Father is?

17
Our Father who art in heaven, / Hallowed be thy name.
(Mt 6:9)

When our Lord was teaching his disciples how to pray, the only name by which he taught them to address God was "Our Father who art in heaven." This surely meant that we were to think of him only in this light. Millions upon millions of times, during all the centuries since, this name has been uttered by the children of God everywhere; and yet how much has it been understood? Had all who used the name known what is meant, it would have been impossible for misrepresentations of his character and doubts of his love and care to have crept in. Tyranny, and unkindness, and neglect, might perhaps be attributed to a God whose name was only king, or judge, or lawgiver. But no such thing could be believed of a God, who is before all else a Father, and, of necessity, since he is God, a good Father. Moreover, since he is an "everlasting Father," he must in the very nature of things act, always and under all circumstances, as a good father ought to act, and never in any other way. It is inconceivable that a good father could forget or neglect or be unfair to his children. A savage father might, or a wicked father, but a good father never! And in calling our God by the blessed name of Father, we ought to know that his fatherhood must be the highest ideal of fatherhood of which we can conceive. It is a fatherhood that combines both father and mother in one, in our highest ideals of both, and comprises all the love, and all the tenderness, and all the compassion, and all the yearning, and all the self-sacrifice, that we cannot but recognize to be the inmost soul of parentage, even though we may not always see it carried out by all earthly parents.

18 *Moses my servant is dead; now therefore arise, go over this Jordan, you and all this people, into the land which I am giving to them, to the people of Israel. (Jos 1:2)*

That Moses could not enter the promised land seems to me to indicate that the law can have nothing to do with the soul that is "seated in heavenly places in Christ Jesus." Moses was in a very special way the representative of the law, as we are told in the Gospel of John: "The law was given through Moses; grace and truth came through Jesus Christ." To make the picture complete, we may well believe that Moses must die before Joshua could lead the people in. The very opening of the Book of Joshua implies this.

It may seem strange to insist upon a perfect obedience to the law and then to talk about the law being dead. But it is a fact in experience that complete surrender to any law always makes the soul free from that law. The law-abiding citizen who has no thought of breaking the laws of his country is as free from those laws as though there were none. The law is dead as far as he is concerned, because it demands only that which he himself thinks is best and right, and which therefore he *wants* to give; and for him in effect there is no law.

19 *Beloved, we are God's children now; it does not yet appear what we shall be, but we know that when he appears we shall be like him, for we shall see him as he is. And every one who thus hopes in him purifies himself as he is pure.*

(1 Jn 3:2-3)

Notice how invariably all the exhortations to holiness are based upon an assured knowledge of our position as the children of God.

We are not called upon to forgive one another in order to induce Christ to forgive us, but we are to forgive others, because we first know that he has already forgiven us. We are not commanded to be followers of God in order to become his children, but because we know we are his children.

A man cannot act like a king unless he knows that he is a king; and similarly we cannot act like the sons and daughters unless we know that we belong to him. In fact, the knowledge of our position and standing is the essential foundation of everything else in the Christian life.

20 *Father, hallowed be thy name. Thy kingdom come. Give us each day our daily bread.* (Lk 11:2-3)

Good commonsense must tell us that our souls need daily food just as much as our bodies. If it is a law in physical life that we must eat to live, it is also equally a law in spiritual life.

"Give us each day our daily bread," is a prayer that includes the soul as well as the body, and unless the religion of Christ contains this necessary food for our weekday lives, as well as for our Sunday lives, it is a grievous failure. But this it does. It is full of principles that fit into human life, as it is in its ordinary commonplace aspects; and the soul that would grow strong must feed itself on these, as well as on the more dainty fare of sermons and services and weekly celebrations.

It is also of vital importance that we choose the right sort of spiritual food upon which to feed. If unwholesome physical food injures physical health, so also must unwholesome mental food injure spiritual health. There is such a thing as spiritual indigestion, just as there is physical indigestion. The laws of spiritual hygiene are as real and as inexorable as the laws of physical hygiene, and it is of vital importance to our soul's health that we should realize this.

21 *They tested God in their heart / by demanding the food they craved.... Therefore, when the Lord heard, he was full of wrath.* (Ps 78:18, 21)

The "wrath of God" is only another name for the inevitable results of our own bad actions. God's wrath is never, as human wrath generally is, an arbitrary condition of the mind, resulting from displeasure at being crossed; but it is simply the necessary result of a broken law, the inevitable reaping of that which has been sown. If a man eats unsuitable food, he will have indigestion. An untaught savage might say that it was the wrath of God that had brought the indigestion upon him, but we, who understand the laws of health, know that his indigestion is simply the necessary result of the unsuitable food he has eaten. Similarly the sickly spiritual condition of so many Christians is not, as they sometimes think, a direct infliction of God's displeasure, but simply and only the necessary consequence of the unsuitable and indigestible spiritual food upon which they have been feeding.

22 *I am the bread of life; he who comes to me shall not hunger, and he who believes in me shall never thirst.*
(Jn 6:35)

To many people this is a very mysterious passage, and I do not at all feel competent to explain it theologically. But is has a commonsense side as well, which has a very practical application to one's everyday life, and it is of this side I want to speak.

Very few persons realize the effect of thought upon the condition of the soul, that it is in fact its food, the substance from which it evolves its strength and health and beauty, or upon which it may become weak and unhealthy and deformed. The things we think about are the things we feed upon. If we think low and corrupt thoughts, we bring diseases upon our soul, just as truly as we bring sickness upon our body by eating corrupt and improper food. The man who thinks about self and feeds on self, may at last become puffed up with self and suffer from the dreadful disease of self-conceit and self-importance. On the other hand, if we think of Christ, we feed on Christ; we eat his flesh and blood practically, by filling our souls with believing thoughts of him.

The Jews said, "How can this man give us his flesh to eat?" A great many people say the same today. I think my suggestions will show one way at least in which he can give it; and I know that any who try this plan of filling their souls with believing thoughts of Christ will find practically that they do feed upon him, to the joy and delight of their hearts.

23 *Finally, brethren, whatever is true, whatever is honorable, whatever is just, whatever is pure, whatever is lovely, whatever is gracious, if there is any excellence, if there is anything worthy of praise, think about these things. (Phil 4:8)*

The things we think about are the things that feed our souls. If we think about pure and lovely things, we shall grow pure and lovely like them; and the converse is equally true. Very few people realize this. Consequently, there is a great deal of carelessness, even with careful people, in regard to their thoughts. They guard their words and actions with the utmost care, but their thoughts, the very spring and root of everything in character and life, they neglect entirely. So long as it is not put into spoken words, it seems of no consequence at all what goes on within the mind. No one hears or knows, and therefore they imagine that the vagrant thoughts that come and go as they please, do no harm. Hence, from carelessness about the books they read or the company they keep, they may be continually imbibing as their soul's food the objectionable ideas of the unbeliever, or the sensualist, or the worldly-minded, or the agnostic, or the Pharisee. It is not possible to carry this on for any length of time without inducing soul-diseases. Gradually all delicate distinctions between faith and unfaith, good and evil, purity and impurity, are more and more obliterated. The soul feeds itself on doubt instead of faith, or on coarseness instead of refinement, and becomes correspondingly bewildered.

24
They said to him, "Lord, give us this bread always."
(Jn 6:34)

If we join in the disciples' prayer, Jesus can only reply to us as he did to them, "Here I am: I am the bread of life; come to me, believe in me, feed your souls with faith in me and with my thoughts." We must do with him as we would with any great master in art or science, whose spirit we wished to assimilate, and whose works we wished to copy. We must study his life, and try to understand his spirit, and imbue ourselves with his ideas. We must, in short, make him our constant mental companion; we must abide with him and in him, and let him abide in us. We must let the underlying thoughts of our heart, at the bottom of all other thoughts, be of the Lord and of all his goodness and his love; and all we do and all we think must be founded on these thoughts concerning him.

25
I am not ashamed, for I know whom I have believed, and I am sure that he is able to guard until that Day what has been entrusted to me. (2 Tm 1:12)

Paul knew Jesus, and therefore Paul could trust him; and if we would trust him as Paul did, we must know him as intimately. I am afraid a great many people are so taken up with Christian doctrines and dogmas, and are so convinced that their salvation is secured because their "views" are sound and orthodox, that they have never yet come to a personal acquaintance with Christ himself. While knowing a great deal about him, they do not know him personally at all. They have a sort of religion that will do for church going or for Sunday work, but they have nothing that will do for their weekday living: "For I desired mercy, and not sacrifice; and the knowledge of God more than burnt offerings" (Hos 6:6).

26 *Now when Jesus came into the district of Caesarea Philippi, he asked his disciples, "Who do men say that the Son of man is? ... Who do you say that I am?" (Mt 16:13, 15)*

This question is of vital importance to each one of us. It becomes a question that each one can and must answer personally and individually for himself. If it were doctrines only that were in question, we might find it necessary to appeal to the creeds and dogmas of our own particular sect or denomination in order to find out just what we do believe, or at least ought to believe. But when it is our personal estimate of our Lord and Master that is in question, we can surely, each one of us, discover very easily what our individual thoughts about him are; what is our own opinion of his character and his ways; what sort of a person, in short, we really think him to be. Is he kind and loving, or is he harsh and severe? Is he trustworthy? Is he sympathetic? Is he true to his promises? Is he faithful? Is he self-sacrificing? Is he full of compassion, or is he full of condemnation? Is he our tender brother, or is he our hard task-master? Does he care most about himself, or about us? Is he on our side, or against us? It is by our answers to questions like these that we shall reveal what our real estimate of Christ is.

27 *Because he cleaves to me in love, I will deliver him; / I will protect him, because he knows my name. (Ps 91:14)*

To "know his name" does not mean to know that he was called Christ or Jesus, but it means to know his character. God's namings always mean character. They are never arbitrary, as our namings are, having no connection with the work or character of the one named. They are always revelations. They tell us what the person is or what he does. "You shall call his name Jesus, for he shall save his people from their sins"; Jesus means Savior.

Continually we find the Lord calling upon the people not to profane his name, that is, not to live and act and talk in such a way as to give others a false idea of his character and his works. And continually we find the saints of all ages calling upon the people to "praise his name," which is evidently equivalent to praising God himself. "Both young men and maidens; old men and children; let them praise the name of the Lord; for His name is excellent."

28 *I will be their God, / and they shall be my people. / And they shall not teach every one his fellow / or every one his brother, saying, "Know the Lord," / for all shall know me, / from the least of them to the greatest.* (Heb 8:10-11)

An essential part of the new covenant is that "all should know him from the least to the greatest." God's part is to reveal himself; our part is to believe his revelations. It is very simple. He tells us he is the Good Shepherd; we are to believe that he actually is, and are to accept him as our Shepherd. He tells us he is the Savior who saves here and now, and we are to believe that it is really true, and are to accept his salvation. Of every revelation he has made of himself in the Bible, we are to say, "This is true." We are simply to lay aside all our own preconceived ideas, and are to accept God's ideas instead. We are to answer the question, "What do you think of Christ?" by replying, "I think of him what the Bible tells me to think, and I think absolutely nothing else."

29 *Do not yield your members to sin as instruments of wickedness, but yield yourselves to God as men who have been brought from death to life, and your members to God as instruments of righteousness.* (Rom 6:13)

To yield anything means simply to make over that thing to the care and keeping of another. To yield ourselves to the Lord, therefore, is to make ourselves over to him, give him the entire possession and control of our whole being. It means to abandon ourselves, to take hands off of ourselves. The word consecration is often used to express this yielding, but I hardly think it is a good substitute. With many people, to consecrate themselves seems to convey the idea of doing something very self-sacrificing, and very good and grand; and it therefore admits of a subtle form of self-glorification. But "yielding" conveys a far more humbling idea; it implies helplessness and weakness, and the glorification of another rather than of ourselves.

30 *Blessed is the man who trusts in the Lord, / whose trust is the Lord. / He is like a tree planted by water, / that sends out its roots by the stream.* (Jer 17:7-8)

I might multiply passages concerning trust indefinitely, for the Bible is simply full of them. The word *believe* is often used instead of the word *trust*, but the idea is the same. In the New Testament, especially, the word *believe* is the one generally used; but this does not mean believing in doctrines or believing in history, but, rather, believing in a person, or, in other words, trusting that person. Christ always said, "Believe in me," not, "Believe this or that about me," but "Believe in me, in me as a Savior who can save." You cannot very well trust in "doctrines" or "plans," no matter how much you may believe in them, but you can always trust in the Lord, whether or not you understand his plans or the doctrines concerning him.

31 *They were stoned, they were sawn in two, they were killed with the sword; they went about in skins of sheep and goats, destitute, afflicted, ill-treated—of whom the world was not worthy—wandering over deserts and mountains, and in dens and caves of the earth.* (Heb 11:37-38)

The next time we are tempted, let us remember that those "of whom the world was not worthy" were tempted also, and we shall not be so discouraged. Discouragement is the very worst thing with which to meet temptation. If we are afraid of falling, we are almost sure to fall. A very wise writer on Christian experience once said that in order to overcome temptation a cheerful confidence that we shall overcome is the first thing, and the second thing, and the third thing, and the thing all the way through. The power of temptation lies largely in the fainting of our own hearts. The children of Israel were continually warned against this. No matter how terrible their enemies seemed, God's word always was, "Dread not, neither be afraid of them." And the reason given was invariably the same, "The Lord shall fight for you, and you shall hold your peace" (see Ex 14:12-14; Dt 1:20-30).

The Lord fights for us now just as he fought for the Israelites then; and we have no more business to be discouraged about our enemies than they had. We see clearly that it was no sin for them to have enemies to fight, and we ought to see as clearly that it is no sin for us. Temptation, therefore, is under no circumstances to be regarded as a sin.

August

1 *Examine yourselves, to see whether you are holding to your faith.* (2 Cor 13:5)

No subject connected with the Christian life has been the cause of more discomfort and suffering to tender consciences than has this subject of self-examination. It has been so constantly impressed upon us that it is our duty to examine ourselves, that the eyes of most of us are continually turned inward, and our gaze is fixed on our own interior states and feelings to such an extent, that self, and not Christ, has come at last to fill the whole horizon.

We ask ourselves an endless number of questions. Am I earnest enough? Have I repented enough? Have I the right sort of feelings? Are my prayers fervent enough? Is my interest in religious things as great as it ought to be? Do I love God with enough fervor? Is the Bible as much of a delight to me as it is to others? All these, and a hundred more questions about ourselves and our experiences, fill up all our thoughts, and sometimes our little self-examination books as well; and day and night we think of the personal pronouns "I," "me," "my," to the utter exclusion of any thought concerning Christ, or any word concerning "he," "him," "his."

When Paul exhorts the Corinthians to examine themselves, he is addressing people guilty of backsliding, telling them to settle definitely whether or not they are still belivers. Paul does not say examine whether you have the right feelings, or whether you motives are pure, but simply and only whether you are "holding to your faith." In short, do you believe in Christ or do you not? A simple question that requires only a simple straightforward answer, yes or no. This is what it meant for the Corinthians, then, and it is what it means for us now.

2 *Watch therefore—for you do not know when the master of the house will come, in the evening, or at midnight, or at cockcrow, or in the morning.* (Mk 13:35)

What are the servants to watch for? Themselves? No, they are to watch for him. We can imagine a servant, instead of watching for the return of his master, spending his time morbidly analyzing his own past conduct, trying to discover whether he had been faithful enough, and becoming so absorbed in self-examination that he lets the master's call go unheeded, and the master's return unnoted. It is the same with the Christian who has formed the mistaken habit of watching and looking at self, instead of watching and looking at Christ.

God says, "Look to me, and you shall be saved," but the self-analyzing soul says, "I must look to myself, if I am to have any hope of being saved. It must be by getting myself right that salvation comes." The phrase "looking to Jesus" is generally acknowledged as one of the watchwords of Christianity. But, after saying this, how many of us go on our old way of self-introspection, trying to find some salvation in ourselves, our feelings, our works of righteousness, and are continually plunged into despair because we never find it?

3 *And when they lifted up their eyes, they saw no one but Jesus only. (Mt 17: 8)*

I was greatly helped many years ago by the following advice: "For one look at self take ten looks at Christ." It was entirely contrary to all I had previously thought right; but it carried conviction to my soul, and delivered me from a habit of morbid self-examination and introspection that had made my life miserable for years. It was an unspeakable deliverance. My experience since leads me to believe that an even better motto would be, "Take no looks at self at all, but look only and always at Christ."

4 *My eyes are ever toward the Lord, / for he will pluck my feet out of the net. (Ps 25:15)*

As long as our eyes are towards our own feet, and towards the net in which they are entangled, we only get into worse tangles. But when we keep our eyes fixed on the Lord, he plucks our feet out of the net. This is a point in practical experience that I have tested hundreds of times, and I know it is a fact. No matter what sort of a snarl I may have been in, whether inward or outward, I have always found that, while I kept my eyes on the snarl, and tried to unravel it, it grew worse and worse; but, when I turned my eyes away from the snarl, and kept them fixed on the Lord, he always, sooner or later, unraveled it and delivered me.

5 *One thing I do, forgetting what lies behind and straining forward to what lies ahead, I press on toward the goal for the prize of the upward call of God in Christ Jesus. (Phil 3:13-14)*

Have you ever watched a farmer plowing a field? If so, you will have noticed that, in order to make straight furrows, he is obliged to fix his eye on a tree or a post in the fence or some object at a farther side of the field, and to guide his plow unwaveringly toward that object. If he begins to look back at the furrow behind him in order to see whether he has made a straight furrow, his plow begins to jerk from side to side, and the furrow he is making becomes a zigzag. If we would make straight paths with our feet, we must do what the Apostle says he did: we must forget the things that are behind and press on toward the goal for the prize of the upward call of God in Christ Jesus. To forget the things that are behind is an essential part of pressing forward towards the prize of our high calling; and I am convinced this prize can never be reached, unless we will consent to this forgetting. When we do consent to it, we come near to putting an end to all our self-examination.

6 *These all look to thee, / to give them their food in due season.* (Ps 104: 27)

We complain of spiritual hunger, and torment ourselves to know why our hunger is not satisfied. Having our eyes upon ourselves and on our own hunger will never bring a supply of spiritual food. When a man's larder is empty and he is starving, he does not spend time looking at the emptiness of his larder. Instead, he looks to the source from which he hopes or expects to get a supply of food. To examine self is to be like a man who spent his time examining his empty larder, instead of going to the market for a supply to fill it. No wonder some Christians seem to be starving to death in the midst of all the fullness there is for them in Christ. They never see that fullness, for they never look at it. They cry out, "O Lord, reveal yourself"; but, instead of looking at God, they look at themselves, and keep their gaze steadily fixed on their own feelings, and then wonder at the "mysterious dealings" of God, in hiding his face from them.

The prophet reproaches the children of Israel, telling them that they "set up their abominations in the house which is called by God's name." When Christians spend their time minutely examining their own condition, raking up all their sins, and bemoaning their shortcomings, what is this but to set up the "abomination" of their own sinful self upon the chief pedestal in their hearts, and to make it the center of their whole religious life, and of all their care and efforts? They gaze at this great, big, miserable self until it fills their whole horizon, and they lose sight of the Lord completely.

7   *Behold, the Lamb of God, who takes away the sin of the world!* (Jn 1:29)

We are never anywhere commanded to behold our emotions, nor our experiences, nor even our sins, but we are commanded to turn our backs upon all these, and to behold the Lamb of God, who takes away our sins. One look at Christ is worth more for salvation than a million looks at self; and yet, so mistaken are our ideas, we seem unable to avoid thinking that self-examination must have in it some saving power, because it makes us so miserable. We have to travel a long way on our heavenly journey before we fully learn that there is no saving power in misery and that a cheerful, confident faith is the only successful attitude for the aspiring soul.

8   *For the love of Christ controls us, because we are convinced that one has died for all; therefore all have died. And he died for all, that those who live might live no longer for themselves but for him who for their sake died and was raised.* (2 Cor 5:14-15)

All through the Bible we are taught this lesson of death to self and life in Christ alone. We tell Christ, "You are all I want." But as a matter of fact we really want a great many other things. We want spiritual "successes" and experiences. And we wonder continually at our failures. But there is no healing or transforming power in gazing at our failures. The only road to Christlikeness is to behold, not our own hatefulness, but his goodness and beauty. We grow like what we look at, and if we spend our lives looking at our hateful selves, we shall become more and more hateful. Beholding self, we are more and more changed into the image of self. If we spend our time beholding the glory of the Lord, that is, letting our minds dwell upon his goodness, and his love, and trying to dwell in his Spirit, the inevitable result will be that we shall be, slowly but surely, changed into the image of the Lord upon whom we are gazing.

9 *"Yet once more I will shake not only the earth but also the heaven." This phrase, "Yet once more," indicates the removal of what is shaken, as of what has been made, in order that what cannot be shaken may remain. (Heb 12:26-27)*

It might seem to those who do not understand the deepest ways of love, that no trials or hardness could ever come into the lives of God's children. But if we look deeply into the matter, we shall see that often love itself must bring the hardness. "The Lord disciplines him whom he loves, and chastises every son whom he receives" (Heb 12:6).

If love sees those it loves going wrong, it must, because of this very love, do what it can to save them; and the love that fails to do this is only selfishness. Therefore, the God of love, when he sees his children resting their souls on things that can be shaken, must necessarily remove those things from their lives, in order that they may be driven to rest only on the things that cannot be shaken; and this process of removing is sometimes very hard.

10 *Every one who hears these words of mine and does not do them will be like a foolish man who built his house upon the sand; and the rain fell, and the floods came, and the winds blew and beat against that house, and it fell; and great was the fall of it. (Mt 7:26-27)*

If our souls are to rest in peace and comfort, it can only be on unshakable foundations. No one can rest comfortably in a shaking bed, or sit in comfort on a rickety chair.

To be reliable, foundations must always be unshakable. The house of the foolish man, which is built on the sand, may present a very fine appearance in clear and sunshiny weather; but when storms arise, and the winds blow, and floods come, that house will fall, and great will be the fall of it. The wise man's house, on the contrary, is built on the rock and is able to withstand all the stress of the storm.

It is possible in the Christian life to build one's spiritual house on such insecure foundations that when storms beat upon it, the ruin of that house is great. Many a religious experience that has seemed fair enough when all was going well in life has tottered and fallen when trials have come, because its foundations have been insecure. It is therefore of vital importance to each one of us to see to it that our Christian life is built upon "things that cannot be shaken."

11   *The Lord is my rock, and my fortress, and my deliverer, / my God, my rock, in whom I take refuge.*
(2 Sm 22:2)

We Christians pay lip sevice to the fact that Christ is the only rock upon which to build. But practically, perhaps unconsciously, we do our best to build on things other than Christ. For instance, we think we must have just the right feelings or the right doctrines or dogmas. If we were perfectly honest with ourselves, I suspect we would often find that we depend almost entirely upon these additions of our own rather than on Christ. If we are to build upon the rock of Jesus Christ, we must once and for all realize that the Lord is enough for our salvation—our Creator and Redeemer, and our all-sufficient portion.

The "foundation of God stands sure," and it is the only foundation that does. Therefore we need to be "shaken" loose from every other foundation so that we may be forced to rest on the foundation of God alone. This explains the necessity for those "shakings" through which so many Christians seem called to pass. Not in anger, but in tenderest love, God shakes our earth and our heaven, until all that "can be shaken" is removed, and only those "things which cannot be shaken" are left behind.

12 *Let us be grateful for receiving a kingdom that cannot be shaken.* (Heb 12: 28)

Hebrews tells us that the things that are shaken are the "things that are made." This is true of the things that are manufactured by our own efforts, the feelings that we get up, doctrines that we elaborate, good works that we perform. These are not bad things in themselves. But when the soul begins to rest on them instead of upon the Lord, he is compelled to "shake" us from them.

There are times when our experience seems to us as settled and immovable as the roots of the everlasting mountains. But there comes an upheaval, and all our foundations are shaken and thrown down, and we are ready to despair, and to question whether we can be Christians at all. Sometimes it is an upheaval in our outward circumstances, and sometimes it is in our inward experience. If people have rested on their good works and their faithful service, the Lord is often obliged to take away all power for work or else all opportunity, in order that the soul may be driven from its false resting place, and forced to rest in the Lord alone. Only God's kingdom cannot be shaken.

13 *Let not him that is deceived trust in vanity: for vanity shall be his recompense.* (Jb 15:31, KJV)

We are told that if we "trust in vanity," vanity shall be our recompense; and many times we have found this to be true. Have you ever crossed a dangerous swamp full of quicksand, where every step was a risk, and where firm-looking ground continually deceived you into a false dependence, causing you to sink in the mire and water concealed beneath its deceptive appearances? If you have, you will be able to understand what it means to "trust in vanity," and you will appreciate the blessedness of anything that shows you the rottenness of your false dependencies and shall drive you to trust in that which is safe and permanent. When our feet are walking on miry clay, we can have nothing but welcome for the divine guide who shall bring us out from the clay, and shall "set our feet upon a rock," and "establish our goings," even though the ways in which he calls us to walk may seem narrow and hard.

14 *By faith Abraham obeyed when he was called to go out to a place which he was to receive as an inheritance.... For he looked forward to the city which has foundations, whose builder and maker is God.* (Heb 11:8, 10)

In order to reach the "city which has foundations," we must go out like Abraham from all other cities, and must be detached from every earthly tie. Everything in Abraham's life that could be shaken was shaken. He was emptied from vessel to vessel, all his resting-places disturbed, and no settlement or comfort anywhere. Like Abraham, we are looking for a city that has foundations, whose builder and maker is God, and therefore we, too, will need to be emptied from vessel to vessel. But we do not realize this, and when the overturnings and shakings come, we are in despair, and think we shall never reach the city at all. But it is these very shakings that make it possible for us to reach it. The psalmist had learned this, and after all the shakings and emptyings of his eventful life, he cried, "For God alone my soul waits in silence, / for my hope is from him. / He only is my rock and my salvation, / my fortress; I shall not be shaken. / On God rests my deliverance and my honor; / my mighty rock, my refuge is God." At last God was everything to him; and then he found that God was enough.

15 *We will not fear though the earth should change, / though the mountains shake in the heart of the sea.... There is a river whose streams make glad the city of God, / the holy habitation of the Most High. / God is in the midst of her, she shall not be moved.* (Ps 46:2, 4-5)

"She shall not be moved"—what an inspiring declaration! Can it be possible that we, who are so easily moved by the things of earth, can arrive at a place where nothing can upset our temper or disturb our calm? Yes, it is possible; and the Apostle Paul knew it. When he was on his way to Jerusalem, where he foresaw that "bonds and afflictions" awaited him, he could say triumphantly, "But none of these things move me." Everything in Paul's life and experience that could be shaken had been shaken, and he no longer counted his life, or any of life's possessions, dear to himself. If we will but let God have his way with us, and come to the same place, neither the little things of life nor the great and heavy trials can have power to move us from the peace that passes understanding.

16 *Therefore let us be grateful for receiving a kingdom that cannot be shaken, and thus let us offer to God acceptable worship, with reverence and awe; for our God is a consuming fire.* (Heb 12:28)

A great many people are afraid of the consuming fire of God, but that is only because they do not understand what it is. The fire of God's love must, in the very nature of things, consume everything that can harm his people; and if our hearts are set on being what the love of God would have us be, his fire is something we shall not be afraid of, but shall eagerly welcome.

Let us thank God that the consuming fire of his love will not cease to burn until it has refined us as silver is refined. For the promise is that he shall sit as a refiner and purifier of silver, and he shall purge us as gold and silver are purged, in order that we may offer him an offering in righteousness. If we will but submit to this purifying process, we are told that we will become pleasing to the Lord, and all nations will call us blessed.

To be pleasing to the Lord may seem impossible when we consider our shortcomings and our unworthiness. But when we think of this lovely consuming fire of God's love, we can be of good heart and take courage, for he will not fail or be discouraged until all our dross and reprobate silver is burned up, and we ourselves come forth in his likeness and conformed to his image.

17 *The soul of the people was much discouraged because of the way.* (Nm 21:4, KJV)

The church of Christ abounds in people who are "discouraged because of the way." Either inwardly or outwardly things look all wrong, and there seems no hope of escape. Their souls faint in them, and their spiritual lives are full of discomfort and misery. There is nothing that more continually and successfully invites defeat. The secret of failure or success in any matter lies far more in the soul's interior attitude than in any other cause or causes. It is a law of our being, that the inward man counts for far more in every conflict than anything the outward man may do or may possess.

Nowhere is this more true than in the spiritual life. Again I must repeat what I find it necessary to say so continually, that the Bible declares from beginning to end, that faith is the law of the spiritual life, and that according to our faith it shall be done to us. Since faith and discouragement cannot, in the very nature of things, exist together, it is perfectly obvious that discouragement must be an absolute barrier to faith. Where discouragement rules, the converse to the law of faith must rule also, and it shall be done to us, not according to our faith, but according to our discouragement. In fact, just as courage is a faith in good, so discouragement is a faith in evil; and, while courage opens the door to good, discouragement opens it to evil.

18 *But I will hope continually, / and will praise thee yet more and more.* (Ps 71:14)

An old saying goes like this: "All discouragement is from the devil." I believe this is a far deeper and more universal truth than we have yet fully understood. Discouragement cannot have its source in God. The religion of the Lord Jesus Christ is a religion of faith, of good cheer, of courage, of hope. "Be discouraged," says our lower nature, "for the world is a place of temptation and sin." "Be of good cheer," says Christ, "for I have overcome the world."

There cannot possibly be any room for discouragement in a world which Christ has overcome.

19 *Moses said to the Lord, "Oh, my Lord, I am not eloquent, either heretofore or since thou hast spoken to thy servant; but I am slow of speech and of tongue. . . . send, I pray, some other person."* (Ex 4:10, 13)

The Lord had called Moses to lead the children of Israel out of the land of Egypt; and Moses, looking at his own natural infirmities and weaknesses, was discouraged. He tried to excuse himself by saying that he was not eloquent and that no one would listen to him. Naturally, one might think that Moses had plenty of cause for discouragement, and for the kind of discouragement most likely to assail us. Like Moses, we distrust our own eloquence, or our own power to convince those to whom we are to be sent; we shrink from the work to which the Lord may be calling us. But notice how the Lord answered Moses. He did not do what Moses would probably have liked best: try to convince him that he really was eloquent, or that his tongue was not slow of speech. He passed all this by, as of no account whatever, and simply called attention to the fact that, since he had made man's mouth and would himself be with the mouth he had made, there could not possibly be any cause for discouragement, even if Moses did have all the infirmities of speech of which he had complained. "Then the Lord said to him, 'Who has made man's mouth? Who makes him dumb, or deaf, or seeing, or blind? Is it not I, the Lord? Now therefore go, and I will be with your mouth and teach you what you shall speak.'"

20 *And the Lord turned to him [Gideon] and said, "Go in this might of yours and deliver Israel from the hand of Midian; do not I send you?"* (Jgs 6:14)

The Lord had called Gideon to deliver his people from the oppression of the Midianites. But Gideon was a poor unknown man, of no family or position and of no apparent fitness for such a great mission. Looking at himself and his own deficiencies, he naturally became discouraged and said, "Pray, Lord, how can I deliver Israel? Behold, my clan is the weakest in Manasseh, and I am the least in my family." Other men, he felt, who had power and influence, might perhaps accomplish this great work, but not one so poor and insignificant as himself. How familiar this sort of talk must sound to anyone who has been a victim of discouragement. How sensible and reasonable it seems. But what did the Lord think of it? "And the Lord said to him, 'But I will be with you, and you shall smite the Midianites as one man.'" God says only, *I will be with you.* Not one word of encouragement does he give Gideon—nor us—about our own capacities or fitness for the work required, but merely the bare statement of the fact, as though it is sufficient for all possible needs. To all words of discouragement this is the invariable answer: *I will be with you.* It is an answer that precludes all possibility of argument or of any further discouragement. I, your Creator and your Redeemer; I, your strength and your wisdom; I, your omnipresent and omniscient God—I will be with you and will protect you through everything; no enemy shall hurt you, no strife of tongues shall disturb you; my presence shall be your safety and your sure defense.

21 *Be not afraid of them, / for I am with you to deliver you, / says the Lord.* (Jer 1:8)

A subtle cause of discouragement is to be found in what is called the fear of man. There seems to exist in this world a company of beings called *they* who rule over life with an iron hand of control. What will *they* say? What will *they* think? These are among the most frequent questions that assail the timid soul when it seeks to work for the Lord. At every turn this omnipotent and ubiquitous *they* stands in our way to discourage us and make us afraid. This form of discouragement is likely to come under the subtle disguise of consideration for the opinion of others; but it is especially dangerous, because it exalts this *they* into the place of God, and esteems *their* opinions above his promises. The only remedy here, as in all other forms of discouragement, is simply the reiteration of the fact that God is with us. For he has said, "I will never leave you nor forsake you." Therefore, we may boldly say, "The Lord is my helper and I will not fear what man may do to me." How can any heart, however timid, dare to indulge in discouragement, in the face of such assertions as these?

22 *The men of Ai killed about thirty-six men of them, and chased them before the gate . . . and slew them at the descent. . . . Then Joshua rent his clothes and fell to the earth upon his face before the ark of the Lord. (Jos 7:5-6)*

The most common form of discouragement arises from our own failures. This was the kind of discouragement that the children of Israel suffered after their defeat at Ai. They had disobeyed the Lord and therefore could not stand before their enemies. So great was their discouragement that the hearts of the people melted and Joshua tore his clothes and fell to the earth. Discouragement and despair seemed the only proper response after such failure. But evidently the Lord thought otherwise, for he said to Joshua, "Arise, why have you thus fallen upon your face? . . . Up, sanctify the people." The proper thing to do after a failure is not to abandon ourselves to utter discouragement, humble as this may appear, but at once to face the evil and get rid of it, and to once again consecrate ourselves to the Lord. "Up, sanctify yourselves," is always God's command. "Lie down and be discouraged," is always our temptation.

23 *Though your sins are like scarlet, / they shall be as white as snow. (Is 1:18)*

You may ask whether a sense of sin produced by the conviction of the Holy Spirit ought not to cause discouragement. If I recognize myself as a sinner, how can I help being discouraged? To this I answer that the Holy Spirit does not convict us of sin in order to discourage us, but to encourage us.

His work is to show us our sin, not that we may lie down in despair under its power, but that we may get rid of it. A good mother points out the faults of her children in order to help them correct those faults; and the convictions of the Holy Spirit are, in truth, one of our greatest privileges, if we only had the sense to see it; for they mean, not that we are to give up in discouragement, but that we are to be encouraged to believe that deliverance is coming.

A good housewife discovers the stains on her table-linen, not in order that she may throw it aside as no longer fit for use, but in order that she may have it cleansed for future use. If she has a good laundress, she will not be discouraged by the worst of stains. Surely then, when God says to us, "though your sins are like scarlet, they shall be as white as snow," it is pure unbelief on our part to allow ourselves to be discouraged at even the worst of our failures, for God's washing of us must be at least as effective as the washing done by any human laundress.

24 *They spoke against God, saying, / "Can God spread a table in the wilderness?" (Ps 78:19)*

From whatever source it may come, discouragement produces many sad results. One of the worst is that it leads people to complain, to "speak against God." When the children of Israel were discouraged in the wilderness, they "spoke against God" and asked all sorts of God-dishonoring questions. If we examine the causes of the rebellious and complaining thoughts that sometimes beset us, we will find that they always begin in discouragement. The truth is that discouragement always involves a kind of speaking against God. It implies some sort of failure on his part to act the way we think he should. The Israelites wandering in the desert asked whether God could provide a table for them. Our questions about God's power or willingness to help us may seem so reasonable and even humble to us. But they are really a way of speaking against God; such questions are displeasing to him, because they reveal the sad fact that we don't believe in him and trust in his salvation.

25 *They brought to the people of Israel an evil report of the land which they had spied out, saying, "The land, through which we have gone, to spy it out, is a land that devours its inhabitants; and all the people that we saw in it are men of great stature." (Nm 13:32)*

Another grievous quality of discouragement is its contagiousness. Nothing is more catching than discouragement. When the spies sent out by Moses brought back an "evil report" of the promised land and told of the giants there, they so discouraged the people that they wept and refused to go into the land which the Lord had given them, and which they had started out in order to possess.

The evil report that so many Christians bring of their failures and their disappointments in the Christian life is one of the most discouraging things in our life together. The hearts of many young Christians are too often discouraged by their older brethren, who have but little idea of the harm they are doing by their doleful accounts of the trials of the way.

26 *But David encouraged himself in the Lord his God. (1 Sm 30:6, KJV)*

If I am asked how we are to get rid of discouragement, I can only say what I say of so many other wrong spiritual habits, *we must give it up.* It is never worthwhile to argue against discouragement. There is only one argument that can meet it, and that is the argument of God. When David was in the midst of what were perhaps the most discouraging moments of his life, when he had found his city burned, and his wives stolen, and he and the men with him had wept until they had no more power to weep, and when his men, exasperated at their misfortunes, spoke of stoning him, then we are told that he "encouraged himself in the Lord his God." The result was a magnificent victory, in which all that they had lost was more than restored to them. This always will be, and always must be the result of a courageous faith, because faith lays hold of the omnipotence of God.

27 *When they make a long blast with the ram's horn, as soon as you hear the sound of the trumpet, then all the people shall shout with a great shout; and the wall of the city will fall down flat.* (Jos 6:5)

Strange words but true, for it came to pass just as the Lord had said. No one can suppose for a moment that this shout caused the walls to fall. And yet the secret of their victory lay in just this shout. For it was the shout of a faith which dared, on the authority of God's word alone, to claim a promised victory while there were no signs of this victory being accomplished. God treated them according to their faith. When they shouted, he made the walls fall down.

God had declared that he had given them the city, and faith reckoned this to be true. Unbelief might well have said, "It would be better not to shout until the walls do actually fall, for, should there be any failure about it, the men of Jericho will triumph, and we shall bring dishonor on the name of our God." But faith laughed at all such prudential considerations, and, confidently resting on God's word, gave a shout of victory, while yet to the eye of sense that victory seemed impossible. Long centuries afterwards the Holy Spirit thus records this triumph of faith in Hebrews: "By faith the walls of Jericho fell down, after they had been encircled for seven days."

28 *In the world you have tribulation; but be of good cheer, I have overcome the world.* (Jn 16:33)

Jesus says "I *have* overcome," not "I *will* overcome." It is already done, and nothing remains but for us to enter into the power of it. There is a great difference between saying, "the Lord will give" and "the Lord has given." A victory promised in the future may be hindered or prevented by a thousand contingencies, but a victory already accomplished cannot be prevented. When our Lord assures us, not that he will overcome the world, but that he has already done so, he gives us an assured foundation for a shout of the most triumphant victory. Henceforward the forces of sin are a defeated and demoralized foe; and, if we believe the words of Christ, we can meet them without fear, since we have been made more than conquerors through him who loves us.

29 *I know that the Lord has given you the land, and that the fear of you has fallen upon us, and that all the inhabitants of the land melt away before you. (Jos 2:9)*

The secret of victory over sin lies in meeting it, not as a foe that has yet to be conquered, but as an enemy that has already been overcome. Rahab knew that the Lord had given Jericho into the hands of the Israelites, and she told this to the spies sent by Joshua. If we were gifted with eyes that could see the unseen kingdom of evil, I believe we would discover that a terror and faintness have fallen upon all the forces of hell, and that they see, in every man and woman of faith, a sure and triumphant conqueror.

It is because we do not know this secret that we meet our spiritual enemies with such fear and trembling and suffer such disastrous defeats.

A Christian I know, who seemed to struggle in vain against temptation, was told this secret by one who had discovered it. At once she went forth to a fresh battle with the confidence of an already accomplished victory. Of course she was victorious. Afterwards, she said that she could almost hear the voice of the tempter saying as he slunk away, "Alas! the game is up. She has found out the secret. She knows that I have already been beaten, and I am afraid I shall never be able to overcome her again!"

30 *Be sober, be watchful. Your adversary the devil prowls around like a roaring lion, seeking some one to devour. Resist him, firm in your faith. (1 Pt 5:8-9)*

It is no sin to hear the "roarings" of the devil, but it becomes sin if we stop and "roar" with him, or yield to his roarings. It is no sin to hear wicked men swearing along the street: it only becomes sin when we stop and join in with them. An old writer says, "Eye not the temptations, but eye the Lord"; and this expresses a profound truth. I believe it is often unwise even to pray much about our temptations, for the fact of praying keeps our mind fixed on them. The best way is a simple turning of the heart to the Lord, as a child to its mother, looking away from the temptation, and looking to Jesus, leaving him to deal with it as he pleases.

31 *Be of good cheer, I have overcome the world.* (Jn 16:33)

This news is an immense help. We can and should meet temptation as an already-conquered foe. In earthly battles, the defeated army becomes disorganized and surrenders the moment they find out that the opposite side has discovered their defeat. The Civil War in America was prolonged far beyond the necessary time, because the North had not yet found out that the South was defeated. The South knew this and kept up the fight. But the moment the South found that the North had discovered the fact of their defeat, they collapsed without another battle. Sin is for us an already-conquered foe. The Lord Jesus Christ has met and conquered it, and we are, if we only knew it, more than conquerors in him.

September

1 Put on the whole armor of God, that you may be able to stand against the wiles of the devil. For we are not contending against flesh and blood, but against the principalities, against the powers, against the world rulers of this present darkness. (Eph 6:11-12)

Our enemies are "giants" now just as truly as they were in Israel's day. And cities, great as Jericho, with walls as high, confront us in our heavenly pathway. Like the Israelites of old, we have no human weapons with which to conquer them. Our armor, like theirs, must be the whole armor of God. Our shield is the same invisible shield of faith that protected them, and our sword must be, as theirs was, the sword of the Spirit, which is the Word, that is, the promises and declarations of God. When our faith puts on this armor of God, and always takes hold of the sword of the Spirit, and we confront our enemy with a shout of undaunted faith, we cannot fail to conquer the mightiest giant or to take the strongest city.

2 *Then my enemies will be turned back / in the day when I call. / This I know, that God is for me.* (Ps 56:9)

Do you know what the psalmist knew? Do you know that God is for you, and that he will cause your enemies to turn back? If you do, then go out to meet your temptations, singing a song of triumph as you go. Meet your very next temptation in this way. At its first approach, begin to give thanks for the victory. Claim continually that you are more than conqueror through him who loves you, and refuse to be frightened off by any foe. Shout the shout of faith with Joshua and Jehoshaphat and David and Paul. I can assure you that when you shout, all your enemies will fall down dead before you.

3 *The Lord who delivered me from the paw of the lion and from the paw of the bear, will deliver me from the hand of this Philistine.* (1 Sm 17:37)

To most of the Israelites it seemed that David had no chance whatever of conquering the mighty giant Goliath. But looking with the eyes of faith, David stood firm in his faith and convinced Saul to let him stand up against the Philistine. However, Saul could not quite abandon his trust in his own accustomed armor, and he armed David with a helmet of brass and a coat of mail and his own powerful sword. But David soon found this too cumbersome and took it off in favor of the simple weapons that the Lord had blessed before—his staff, his slingshot, and five smooth stones out of the brook. Armed with these, he drew near to the giant.

When the giant saw the youth who had come to fight him, he disdained him, and said contemptuously, "Come to me, and I will give your flesh to the birds of the air and to the beasts of the field." To every eye, it looked like an unequal battle. But David's faith triumphed, and he shouted a shout of victory even before the battle had begun. "You come to me with a sword and with a spear and with a javelin; but I come to you in the name of the Lord of hosts, the God of the armies of Israel, whom you have defied. This day the Lord will deliver you into my hand."

In the face of such faith as this, what could even a giant do? Every word of David's triumphant shout of victory was fulfilled; and the mighty enemy was delivered into the hands of the youth he had disdained.

4 *O give thanks to the Lord, for he is good;/his steadfast love endures forever! (Ps 118:1)*

Thanksgiving or complaining—these words express two contrasting attitudes of the souls of God's children regarding his dealings with them; and they are more powerful than we are inclined to believe, in furthering or frustrating his purposes of comfort and peace towards us. The soul that gives thanks can find comfort in everything; the soul that complains can find comfort in nothing.

5 *Give thanks in all circumstances; for this is the will of God in Christ Jesus for you. (1 Thes 5:18)*

God's command is to give thanks in all circumstances. It is an actual and positive command; and if we want to obey God, we have simply got to give thanks in everything. There is no getting around it.

A great many Christians have never realized this. Although they may be familiar with the command, they have always looked upon it as a sort of counsel of perfection, to which mere flesh and blood could never be expected to attain. Unconsciously, perhaps, they change the wording of the passage and substitute "be resigned" for "give thanks." Instead of "all circumstances," they substitute "a few circumstances." And they entirely leave out the words "for this is the will of God in Christ Jesus for you."

If brought face to face with the actual wording of the command, such Christians will say, "Oh, but it is an impossible command. If everything came directly from God, one might be able to do it, but most things come through human sources, and often are the result of sin." To this I answer that it is true that we cannot always give thanks for the things themselves, but we can always give thanks for God's love and care in the circumstances. He may not have ordered them, but he is in them somewhere, and he is in them to work out even the most grievous situation for our good.

6 I give thee thanks, O Lord, with my whole heart; before the gods I sing thy praise. (Ps 138:1)

It is evident from the whole teaching of scripture that the Lord loves to be thanked and praised just as much as we do. I am sure that it gives him real downright pleasure, just as it does us and that our failure to thank him for his gifts wounds his loving heart, just as our hearts are wounded when our loved ones fail to appreciate the benefits we have so enjoyed bestowing upon them. What a joy it is to receive from our friends an acknowledgment of their thanksgiving for our gifts, and is it not likely that it is a joy to the Lord also?

7 As therefore you received Christ Jesus the Lord, so live in him, rooted and built up in him and established in the faith, just as you were taught, abounding in thanksgiving.
(Col 2:6-7)

Even when we realize that things come directly from God, we find it very hard to give thanks for what hurts us. Do we not, however, all know what it is to thank a skillful physician for his treatment of our diseases, even though that treatment may have been very severe? Surely we should no less give thanks to our Divine Physician, when he is obliged to give us bitter medicine to cure our spiritual diseases, or to perform a painful operation to rid us of something that harms.

Rather than thanking him we complain against him; although we generally direct our complaints, not against the Divine Physician himself, who has ordered our medicine, but against the "bottle" in which he has sent it. This "bottle" is usually some human being whose unkindness, carelessness, neglect, or cruelty has caused our suffering; but who has been after all only the instrument or "second cause" that God has used for our healing.

8 *The people murmured against Moses, saying, "What shall we drink?" (Ex 15:24)*

When the children of Israel found themselves wandering in the wilderness, they complained that Moses had brought them there to kill them with hunger and thirst. But in reality their complaining was against God, for God was really the one who had brought them out of Egypt, not Moses. He was only a "second cause."

We may think, as the Israelites did, that our discomforts and deprivations have come from human hands only, and may therefore feel at liberty to "murmur against" these second causes. But God is the great Cause behind all second causes. The second causes are only the instruments that he uses; and when we murmur against these, we are really murmuring, not against the instruments, but against God himself. Second causes are powerless to act, except by God's permission; and what he permits becomes really his arranging. At bottom, all complaining means just this, that we do not believe in God and do not trust in his salvation.

9 *I will speak in the anguish of my spirit;/I will complain in the bitterness of my soul. (Jb 7:11)*

Job was a great complainer; and we may think, as we read his story, that he had excellent reason to complain. His circumstances seemed to be full of hopeless misery. We can hardly wonder at Job's complaint. And yet, could he but have seen the divine side of all his troubles, he would have known that they were permitted in the tenderest love and were to bring him a revelation of God such as he could have had by no other means. Could he have seen that this was to be the outcome, he would not have uttered a single complaint, but would have given triumphant thanks for the trials which were to bring him such glorious blessing. And could we but see, in our heaviest trials, the end from the beginning, I am sure that thanksgiving would take the place of complaining in every case.

10 *Out of the belly of Sheol I cried, and thou didst hear my voice. . . . I with the voice of thanksgiving will sacrifice to thee; what I have vowed I will pay. Deliverance belongs to the Lord!* (Jon 2:2, 9)

Jonah was a wonderful illustration of this. His prayer of thanksgiving out of the belly of hell is a tremendous lesson.

No depth of misery is too great for the sacrifice of thanksgiving. We cannot, it is true, give thanks for the misery, but we can give thanks to the Lord in the misery, just as Jonah did. No matter what our trouble, the Lord is in it somewhere; and, of course, being there, he is there to help and bless us. Therefore, when our "souls faint within us" because of our troubles, we have only to remember this, and to thank him for his presence and his love.

11 *Good and upright is the Lord; / therefore he instructs sinners in the way. / He leads the humble in what is right, / and teaches the humble his way.* (Ps 25:8-9)

It is not because *things* are good that we are to thank the Lord, but because *he* is good. We are not wise enough to judge things, to know whether they are really, in their essence, joys or sorrows; but we always know that the Lord is good, and that his goodness makes it absolutely certain that everything he provides or permits, must be good; and must therefore be something for which we would be heartily thankful, if only we could see it with his eyes.

12 Enter his gates with thanksgiving, and his courts with praise! / Give thanks to him, bless his name! (Ps 100:4)

We are commanded to enter into God's gates with thanksgiving and into his courts with praise, and I am convinced that the giving of thanks is the key that opens these gates more quickly than anything else. Try it. The next time you feel dead, cold, and low-spirited, begin to praise and thank the Lord. Enumerate to yourself the benefits he has bestowed upon you, and thank him heartily for each one, and see if your spirits do not begin to rise and your heart get warmed up.

Sometimes, you may feel too disheartened to pray; then try giving thanks instead. Before you know it, you will find yourself glad and thankful for all God's loving-kindness and his tender mercies.

13 And when the priests came out of the holy place, a cloud filled the house of the Lord, so that the priests could not stand to minister because of the cloud; for the glory of the Lord filled the house of the Lord. (1 Kgs 8: 10-11)

It is striking to notice how much thanksgiving had to do with the building of the Temple. When they had collected the treasures for the Temple, David gave thanks to the Lord for enabling them to do it. When the Temple was finished, the people gave thanks again. Then a wonderful thing happened— the glory of the Lord filled the Temple. When the people praised and gave thanks, then the house was filled with the glory of the Lord. We may be sure that the reason our hearts are not more often filled with the "glory of the Lord," is because we do not raise our voices often enough in praise and thanksgiving.

14 For those whom he foreknew he also predestined to be conformed to the image of his Son, in order that he might be the first-born among many brethren. (Rom 8:29)

God's ultimate purpose in our creation was that we should finally be "conformed to the image of his Son." Christ was to be the first-born among many brethren, and his brethren were to be like him. All the discipline and training of our lives has this end in view; and God has implanted in every human heart a longing, however unformed and unexpressed, after the best and highest it knows.

When God said in the beginning, "Let us make man in our image, after our likeness," we cannot for a moment suppose that he meant we were to be made in the image and likeness of his body. He must have meant that we were to be made in the image and likeness of his nature and character. Neither could he have meant that we were to be created full-fledged in this image, but that we were to be begun, as all adult life is begun, in helpless and ignorant infancy. God knows what we will become just as an architect knows what his building will become, when as yet only the foundation has been laid.

15 *We are God's children now; it does not yet appear what we shall be, but we know that when he appears we shall be like him, for we shall see him as he is.* (1 Jn 3:2)

Christ is the pattern of what each one of us is to be when finished. We are to be filled with the Spirit of Christ; we are to share his resurrection life and to walk as he walked. We are to be one with him as he is one with the Father; and the glory God gave to him, he is to give to us. When all this is brought to pass, then, and not until then, will God's purpose in our creation be fully accomplished.

Our likeness to Christ is an accomplished fact in the mind of God, but we are, so to speak, still being manufactured, and the great Master Workman is at work upon us.

16 *And we all, with unveiled face, beholding the glory of the Lord, are being changed into his likeness from one degree of glory to another.* (2 Cor 3:18)

In order to be laborers together with God, we must not only build with his materials, but also according to his processes, and of these we are often quite ignorant. Our idea of building is of hard laborious work, done by the sweat of our brow; but God's idea is far different. Paul tells us what it is. Our work is to "behold the glory of the Lord," and, as we behold, the Lord effects the marvelous transformation, and we are changed into his likeness. This means, of course, to behold, not in the earthly sense of merely looking at a thing, but in the divine sense of really seeing the thing. We are to behold with our spiritual eyes the glory of the Lord and are to continue beholding it. The glory of the Lord does not consist, however, of a great shiny halo. The real glory of the Lord is the glory of what he is and what he does, the glory of character. This is what we are to behold.

17 *Do not lie to one another, seeing that you have put off the old nature with its practices and have put on the new nature, which is being renewed in knowledge after the image of its creator.* (Col 3:9)

Sin must disappear when Christ comes in, and no soul that is not prepared to surrender all that is contrary to God's will, can hope to welcome him. The "old nature" must be put off if the new nature is to reign. But both the putting off and the putting on must be done by faith. There is no other way. We must move our personality, our ego, our will, out of self and into Christ. We must count ourselves to be dead to self and alive only to God. The same kind of faith which brings the forgiveness of sins within our grasp, brings also this union with Christ. To those who do not understand the law of faith, this will no doubt be as great a mystery as the secrets of gravitation were before the law of gravitation was discovered. But, to those who understand it, the law of faith works as unerringly and as definitely as the law of gravitation. No one can read the seventh chapter of Hebrews and fail to see that faith is an all-conquering force. I believe myself it is the creative force of the universe. It is the higher law that controls all the lower laws beneath it. What looks like a miracle is simply the working of this higher controlling law.

18 *If you have faith as a grain of mustard seed, you will say to this mountain, "Move from here to there," and it will move; and nothing will be impossible to you.* (Mt 17:20-21)

Faith, we are told, calls those things which are not as though they were, and, in so calling them, brings them into being. Therefore, although we cannot see any tangible sign of change when by faith we put off the old man, which is corrupt, and by faith put on the new man, we really are transformed, and faith has accomplished it. I cannot explain this theologically, but I can fearlessly assert that it is a tremendous practical reality; and that those souls who abandon the self-life and give themselves up to the Lord to be fully possessed by him, do find that he takes possession of the inner springs of their being and works there to will and to do his good pleasure.

19 *You show that you are a letter from Christ delivered by us, written not with ink but with the Spirit of the living God, not on tablets of stone but on tablets of human hearts.* (2 Cor 3:3)

Paul says we are to be "letters of Christ," known and read by all men. If every child of God would begin from this day on to be a "letter of Christ," living a truly Christlike life at home and abroad, it would not be a month before the churches would be overflowing with people who wanted to know what power could so transform human nature into something divine.

The world is full of unbelievers, and nothing will convince them but facts which they cannot disprove. We must meet them with transformed lives. If they see that we were once cross and now kind, once proud and now humble, once fretful and now patient and calm, and if we are able to testify that it is faith in Christ that has accomplished this change, they will not help but be impressed.

20 *You shall be my witnesses in Jerusalem and in all Judea and Samaria and to the end of the earth.* (Acts 1:8)

A cross Christian, an anxious one, a discouraged and gloomy Christian, a doubting Christian, a complaining Christian, an exacting Christian, a selfish, cruel, hard-hearted Christian, a self-indulgent Christian, a Christian, in short, who is not Christlike, may preach to the winds with as much hope of success, as to preach to his own family or friends, who see him as he is. There is no escape from this inevitable law of things, and we may as well recognize it at once. If we want our loved ones to trust the Lord, volumes of talk about it will not be of any help unless we display a little real trust on our own part. The longest prayer and the loudest preaching are of no avail in any family circle, however they may do in the pulpit, unless the preacher lives out the things preached.

21

You, therefore, must be perfect, as your heavenly Father is perfect. (Mt 5:48)

It was no mere figure of speech when our Lord, in that wonderful Sermon on the Mount, said these words to his disciples. He meant, of course, according to our measure, but he meant that we were really to be conformed to his image. It is to be by his working in us, and not by our working in ourselves, that this purpose of God in our creation is to be accomplished; and if it should look to some of us as though we are too far removed from the image of Christ for such a transformation to be possible, we must remember that our Maker is not done with us yet. The day will come, if we do not hinder it, when the work begun in Genesis shall be finished in Revelation, and the whole creation shall be delivered from the bondage of corruption. We will enter into the glorious liberty of the children of God.

22

In the multitude of my thoughts within me thy comforts delight my soul. (Ps 94:19, KJV)

With the psalmist, we must allow God's comfort to delight us. But I am afraid that among the multitude of our thoughts within us, there are far too often many more thoughts of our own discomforts than of God's comforts. We must think of his comforts if we are to be comforted by them. It might be a good exercise of soul for some of us to analyze our thoughts for a few days and see how many thoughts we actually do give to God's comforts, compared to the the number we give to our own discomforts. I think the result would amaze us!

23 *Now to him who by the power at work within us is able to do far more abundantly than all that we ask or think, to him be glory in the church and in Christ Jesus to all generations.* (Eph 3:20-21)

Discomfort and unrest in the spiritual life arise from strenuous but useless efforts to get up some satisfactory basis of confidence within ourselves. The self looks for the "right kind of feelings," or the right amount of fervor or earnestness, or at least a sufficient degree of interest in spiritual matters. Because none of these things are ever satisfactory (and never will be), it is impossible for the spiritual life to be anything but uncomfortable.

If we recognize that all our salvation, from beginning to end, depends on the Lord alone; and if we have learned that he is able and willing to do for us "more abundantly than all we ask or think," then peace and comfort cannot fail to reign supreme. Everything depends upon whether the Lord, in and of himself, is enough for our salvation, or whether we think other things must be added to make him sufficient.

24 *Hallelujah! For the Lord our God the Almighty reigns.*
(Rv 19:6)

Some years ago I was passing through a great deal of questioning and perplexity in my spiritual life. Someone advised me to pay a visit to a particular woman who was thought to be a deeply spiritual Christian. I summoned up my courage and went to see her and poured out my troubles. I expected her to take a deep interest in me and to take great pains to do all she could to help me. She listened patiently enough and did not interrupt me. But when I had finished my story and had paused, expecting sympathy and consideration, she simply said, "Yes, all you say may be very true, but then, in spite of it all, there is God." I waited a few minutes for something more, but nothing came. "But," I continued, "surely you don't understand how very serious and perplexing my difficulties are." "Oh yes, I do," she replied, "but then, as I tell you, there is God."

Her answer seemed to me most disappointing and unsatisfactory. I felt that my experiences could not be met by anything so simple as the statement, "Yes, but there is God." However, my need was so great that I went to her again and again, always with the hope that she would begin to understand the importance of my difficulties and would give me more help. It was of no avail. I was never able to draw forth any other answer. Always to everything would come the simple reply, "Yes, I know, but there is God." At last, I became convinced that my friend really and truly believed that the mere fact of the existence of God, as Creator and Redeemer, was an all-sufficient answer to every possible need of his creatures. Because she said it so often and seemed so sure, I began dimly to wonder whether after all God might be enough, even for my need. From wondering I came gradually to believing, and at last a conviction burst upon me that he really was enough, and my eyes were opened to the fact of the absolute and utter all-sufficiency of God.

25 For all things are yours, whether Paul or Apollos or Cephas or the world of life or death or the present or the future, all are yours; and you are Christ's; and Christ is God's.
(1 Cor 3:21-23)

No statement could be more all-embracing than this one. All things are yours simply because you belong to Christ, not because you are so good or so worthy, but simply and only because you belong to Christ. All the things we need are part of our inheritance in him, and they only await our claiming. Because he is, all must go right for us. Because the mother is, all must go right, up to the measure of her ability, for her children. How much more true this must be of the Lord. While the mother lives, the child must be cared for; and, while God lives, his children must be cared for as well. What else could he do, being who he is?

26 *Though He slay me, yet will I trust in Him.*
                                              (Jb 13:15, KJV)

God's saints in all ages have realized that God was enough for them. Job spoke words of trust which few can equal. David could say in the moment of his worst anguish, "Even though I walk through the valley of the shadow of death, / I fear no evil; / for thou art with me."

Paul could say triumphantly, in the midst of many grievous trials, "For I am sure that neither death, nor life, nor angels, nor principalities, nor things present, nor things to come, nor powers, nor height, nor depth, nor anything else in all creation, will be able to separate us from the love of God in Christ Jesus our Lord."

Therefore, O doubting and sorrowful Christian hearts, in the face of all we have learned concerning the God of all comfort, cannot you realize with Job and David and Paul and the saints of all the ages, that nothing else is needed to quiet all your fears, but just this, that *God is*? Nothing can separate you from his love, absolutely nothing. Every possible contingency is provided for in Paul's words, and not one of them can separate you from the love of God which is in Christ Jesus our Lord.

27 *Have no anxiety about anything, but in everything by prayer and supplication with thanksgiving let your requests be made known to God. And the peace of God, which passes all understanding, will keep your hearts and your minds in Christ Jesus.* (Phil 4:6-7)

Notice the phrase "have no anxiety." It covers all possible grounds for anxiety, both inward and outward. We are continually tempted to think it is our duty to be anxious about some things. Perhaps our thought will be, "Oh yes, it is quite right to give up all anxiety in a general way; and in spiritual matters of course anxiety is wrong; but there *are* things about which it would be a sin not to be anxious—about our children, for instance, or those we love, or about our church affairs and the cause of truth, or about business matters. It would show a great lack of concern not to be anxious about such things as these." Or else our thoughts say, "Yes, it is quite right to commit our loved ones and all our outward affairs to the Lord, but when it comes to our inward lives, our religious experiences, our temptations, our besetting sins, our growth in grace, and all such things, these we *ought* to be anxious about, for if we are not, they will be sure to be neglected."

To such suggestions and to all similar ones, the answer is found in our text: "have no anxiety."

28 *Look at the birds of the air: they neither sow nor reap nor gather into barns, and yet your heavenly Father feeds them. Are you not of more value than they?* (Mt 6:26)

This illustration cannot be misunderstood. The birds are before us continually, as living examples of what real trust is. With them of course it is unconscious trust, but with us it must be an intelligent and conscious act. One who had learned this lesson, thus writes concerning it: "Long years ago I was in the act of kneeling down before the Lord my God, when a little bird in the lightest, freest humor, came and perched near my window, and thus preached to me, all the while hopping from spray to spray, 'Oh thou grave man, look on me and learn something. Thy God made me, and if thou canst conceive it, he loves me, and cares for me. Thou studiest him in great problems which oppress and confound thee, and thou losest sight of one-half of his ways. Learn to see thy God, not in great mysteries only, but in me also. His burden on me is light, his yoke on me is easy, for I have only to submit to him and trust. But thou makest yokes and burdens for thyself, which are grievous to be borne, because thou wilt neither submit nor trust. I advise thee to follow my example, as thy Master commanded thee to do. Consider that the bird and the flower are as really from God as thou art; and that their lives are figures of something which he wants to see in thee also. Behold the fowls of the air, for they sow not, neither do they reap, nor gather into barns; yet your heavenly Father feedeth them.'"

29 *Fear not, for I am with you, / be not dismayed, for I am your God; / I will strengthen you, I will help you, / I will uphold you with my victorious right hand. (Is 41:10)*

The One upon whom our cares are to be cast, is able to bear them, no matter how great they may be. Yet we, who often entrust our most valuable possessions to other human beings and feel no fear, are afraid to trust our Lord.

Think of the blessed confidence with which children cast their cares upon their parents, and recall how the parents love to have it so. How often a mother, when her child is tempted to be anxious or worried over something will say, "There, darling, don't worry; leave it all to me, and I will attend to it. Only trust me, and do as I say, and all will come right." The only thing that a mother asks of her child is that it will yield to her care and obey her voice, and then she will take charge of all the rest. It is the same with us and our God.

30 *Peace I leave with you; my peace I give to you; not as the world gives do I give to you. Let not your hearts be troubled, neither let them be afraid. (Jn 14:27)*

Here the Master *commands* us not to be troubled or afraid. Every time we yield to anxiety or fear we are disobeying him. Three instances are recorded in which our Lord rebuked his disciples for lacking faith. Yet in each case the circumstances seemed to call for anxiety as the only natural and proper response. Similar circumstances would cause great anxiety in many Christian hearts today.

First it was in a storm at sea. A furious storm arose and the disciples feared for their lives. Yet Jesus was aboard and he calmed the waves and told them that they had no reason to be fearful.

The second instance was when Peter found himself sinking in the waters. Jesus reached out to him and held him up but then asked him why he doubted.

The third was when the disciples were troubled because they had no bread to feed the five thousand. Jesus reminds them of past experiences, when he supplied all their needs. Why should they trust him any less now? I am sure he was grieved by the doubts of his disciples, just as we are grieved when those whom we love and whom we are trying to serve are anxious and fearful about the things we have promised them.

October

1 *Then they cried to the Lord in their trouble, / and he delivered them from their distress.* (Ps 107:6)

We are tempted to think that trouble shuts God's ears. In times of prosperity we rejoice to believe he hears us, but when the dark days come, we moan and complain because our prayers do not reach him. Which cry catches the mother's ear the soonest, the cry of joy or the cry of sorrow? There can be but one answer to this. Every mother knows that the happy noises of her children in the nursery often pass by unnoticed, but the slightest cry of pain or trouble reaches her ear at once. Is a mother more alert to the suffering of her children than God?

2 *The eternal God is your dwelling place, / and underneath are the everlasting arms.* (Dt 33:27)

Do we not act sometimes as though we thought we were carrying the Lord, rather than that he was carrying us? And do we not go bowed down under this fancied burden, when we ought to be resting peacefully in his arms? A baby, safe in its mother's arms, will sometimes make little clutches of fright, as though its safety depended upon the strength of its tiny grasp of the mother's neck. But the mother knows how useless these are, and that it is *her* grasp, and not the baby's, that secures its safety. Surely this is true of us in the arms of God.

3 *Like an eagle that stirs up its nest, / that flutters over its young, / spreading out its wings, catching them, / bearing them on its pinions.* (Dt 32:11)

Even the eagle knows this secret of mother love. When the little eagles are old enough to learn to fly, she stirs up the nest and thrusts them out, that they may be driven to find the use of their wings. But she floats in the air under them, and watches them with eyes of love, and when she sees any little eaglet showing signs of weariness, she flies beneath it and spreads out her great strong mother wings to bear it up until it is rested and ready to fly again. And so the Lord.

4 *By this we know love, that he laid down his life for us; and we ought to lay down our lives for the brethren.* (1 Jn 3:16)

All nature teaches us this law of the self-sacrifice of motherhood. Even the wild tiger-mother yields to its power. One writer has said concerning this: "It is a tiger's impulse to resent an injury. Pluck her by the hair, smite her on the flank, she will leap upon and rend you. But to resent an injury is not her strongest impulse. Watch those impotent kitten creatures playing with her. They are so weak, a careless movement of her giant paw would destroy them; but she makes no careless movement. They have caused her a hundredfold the pain your blow produced; yet she does not render evil for evil. These puny mites of helpless impotence she strokes, with love's light in her eyes;

she licks the shapeless forms of her tormentors, and, as they plunge at her, each groan of her anguish is transformed by love into a whinney of delight. She moves her massive head in a way which shows that he, who bade you turn the other cheek, created her. When strong enough to rise, the terrible creature goes forth to sacrifice herself for her own. She will starve that they may thrive. She is terrible for her little ones, as Christ was terrible for his. He who made her, taught her the secret of motherhood."

5 *When the Lord restored the fortunes of Zion, / we were like those who dream. / Then our mouth was filled with laughter, / and our tongue with shouts of joy.* (Ps 126:1-2)

When their captivity was ended, the Israelites rejoiced without any effort. They could not sing songs of joy in the strange land, but as soon as they were at home again, their tongues were filled with singing. And we are like them; we cannot rejoice until we also know that our captivity has been ended; but when we do know it, our mouths, like theirs, are filled with laughter and our tongues with singing, without any effort.

6 *You shall see, and your heart shall rejoice; / your bones shall flourish like the grass.* (Is 66:14)

"You shall see, and your heart shall rejoice." We need to "see" our blessings before we can rejoice over them. The Israelites could see their blessings with their outward eyes, for they were visible and tangible things. But we must see ours with our inward eyes, for they are invisible and spiritual. Our knowledge concerning them can only come by faith, while theirs came by sight. But faith is inward seeing. To believe a thing on sufficient authority is as real as seeing it.

7 *Therefore, since we are justified by faith, we have peace with God through our Lord Jesus Christ. Through him we have obtained access to this grace in which we stand.*
(Rom 5:1-2)

The fact of our forgiveness in Christ is preached to us. We believe the word preached. And as a result we have peace.

But some may ask, "Is the fact true until we believe it? Are my sins forgiven before I believe that they are?" Certainly they are. In the heart of God there is always forgiveness, like the mother, whose forgiveness always awaits the sin of her child. But this forgiveness cannot reach us until we believe in it. Our faith does not induce God to forgive us; it is not in any sense the cause of our forgiveness. Faith is only the hand by which we lay hold experimentally of the forgiveness that is already ours in Christ.

8 *Before the mountains were brought forth, / or ever thou hadst formed the earth and the world, / from everlasting to everlasting / thou art God.* (Ps 90:2)

God alone is unchangeable; what we call spiritual blessings are full of the element of change. The prayer which is answered today may seem to be unanswered tomorrow; the promises, once so gloriously fulfilled, may cease to have any apparent fulfillment; the spiritual blessing, which was at one time such a joy, may be utterly lost; and nothing of all we once trusted and rested on may be left us, but the hungry and longing memory of it all. But when all else is gone, God is still left. Nothing changes him. He is the same yesterday, today, and forever, and in him is no variableness, no shadow of turning. And the soul that finds its joy in him alone can suffer no wavering.

9 *For he has said, "I will never fail you nor forsake you." Hence we can confidently say, / "The Lord is my helper, I will not be afraid; / what can man do to me?"* (Heb 13:5-6)

What God "has said," we may indeed repeat with confidence. Therefore our faith must unswervingly assert that fact of God's abiding presence with us. As a result of this faith we shall sooner or later experience a conscious feeling of his presence. He is not present because we *feel* him to be, but we feel his presence because we *believe* in the fact of it.

This divine order of the three F's, i.e., first fact, second faith, third feeling, applies to every aspect and every stage of our experience in heavenly things.

No amount of feeling is good for anything unless it is the result of faith in a divine fact; which fact is true anyhow, whether we believe it or not. Let us get our facts then. And let us once and for all give up every idea that our feelings are the test and measure of these facts. The facts, when believed in, will control our feelings; but no amount of feeling, no matter how fervent, can control the facts, so much as a feather's weight.

10   *Thou dost keep him in perfect peace, / whose mind is stayed on thee, / because he trusts in thee.* (Is 26:3)

A Christian who had had a very joyous experience in a prayer meeting, came to the minister the next day looking very downcast and said, "In your meeting yesterday I was filled with joy, and I thought I should never be sad again; but now it is all gone and I am in the depths. What is the matter with me? Has God forsaken me?"

"Did you ever pass through a tunnel?" asked the minister. "Certainly I have," replied the man, "but I do not see what that has to do with it." "When you were in the tunnel did you think the sun had been blotted out and existed no longer?" continued the minister. "No, of course I did not," said the man. "I knew the sun was in the sky just the same, although I could not see it just then. But what has that to do with my experience?" "Were you very much depressed while you were going through the dark tunnel?" "No I was not, I knew I should get out into the light again soon." "And did you get out?" asked the minister. "I am out now!" exclaimed the man joyfully. "I see what you mean. The facts are just the same, no matter how I feel, and I am to rejoice in the facts not in my feelings. I see!"

11   *For once you were darkness, but now you are light in the Lord; walk as children of light.* (Eph 5:8)

You *are* children of light, now walk as such. That is, *be* what you *are*. In our relations with God this is especially necessary, because these all exist in the unseen spiritual region, and can of course only be real to us as our faith makes them so. It is essential, then, to our peace, and also to our well-being, that we should intelligently take hold of and live out that for which Christ Jesus took hold of us. That is, we must find out who we are in God's eyes, and then we must *be* just that. For instance, if God says I am his child, then I must *be* his child; if he says I am a king, then I must *be* kingly, and so on in all our relationships with God.

12   *And you are my sheep, the sheep of my pasture, and I am your God, says the Lord God.* (Ez 34:31)

Let us *be* sheep then and abandon ourselves to the care of the Shepherd to whom we belong. The sheep cannot care for themselves, protect themselves, or provide food for themselves; the Shepherd must do it all. The responsibility of their well-being is all on his shoulders, not on theirs. They have nothing to do but to trust him and to follow him.

A great many people refuse to be the sheep and insist upon trying to be the shepherd instead. That is, they try to assume all the duties that belong to the shepherd; and they entirely refuse to be cared for and protected as the sheep are. Or else they try to be both the sheep and also the shepherd, and to perform the part of each at the same time, an impossible and wearisome task. Let us cease, then, trying to be anything but just simply what we are; sheep in the care of the Divine Shepherd.

13   *Abide in me, and I in you. As the branch cannot bear fruit by itself, unless it abides in the vine, neither can you, unless you abide in me.* (Jn 15:4)

Be branches then, and realize that you have no life apart from the vine: and realize also that you have nothing to do in order to bring forth much fruit, but to abide in the vine. The branch cannot bear fruit of itself, in the very nature of things. Do not try, then, to do it, but abide in the vine, and let the life-giving sap flow through you, without effort on your part, and without anxiety. Only see to it that you do not hinder its flow by doubt or by rebellion. *Be* a branch and a branch only, and do not try to be anything else. Do not try to *make* the fruit, but consent to *bear* it. Let it grow.

14   *Consider the lilies of the field, how they grow; they neither toil nor spin; yet I tell you, even Solomon in all his glory was not arrayed like one of these.* (Mt 6:28-29)

Let us be like the lilies of the field and grow as they grow, in a happy unconsciousness of our growing. Let us consider "how they grow," and let us give up all our straining, and stretching, and self-efforts after growth, and try to grow like them by the power of an inward growing-life alone. Let us be like them also in this, that we do not try to cultivate ourselves. Too many try to be their own husbandmen, to cultivate, and water, and dig about, and prune, and even sometimes to plant themselves. They try to be what they are not, and what they never can be, i.e., the husbandman instead of the branches, the gardener instead of the garden, the farmer instead of the trees and flowers. And of course they fail. But let us be what we are, the trees, and flowers, and gardens only, and let us leave to our Divine Husbandman all the care and responsibility of our growing and our blooming.

15 Do not yield your members to sin as instruments of wickedness, but yield yourselves to God as men who have been brought from death to life, and your members to God as instruments of righteousness. (Rom 6:13)

God does not tell us that we are the workmen, who are to use and manage the instruments, but that we are the instruments to be used and managed by the Divine Master Workman who made us, and who alone, therefore, understands for what work we are best fitted. The only thing the instrument can do is to "yield" itself perfectly to the will of the Master Workman. The Master surely knows how best to use his instruments, and it is plainly not the business of the tool to decide these questions for itself. Neither must it try to help by its own efforts to do the work. One absolutely necessary characteristic of a tool is its pliableness. The moment resistance is felt in any tool, the moment it refuses to move just as the master wants, that moment it becomes unfit for use. If I am writing, and my fine gold pen begins to leak and to move with difficulty, I will soon lay it aside and take gladly in its place even a stub end of a lead pencil, if only it will move easily in obedience to my will. The strength of an instrument lies in its helplessness. Because it is helpless to do anything of itself, therefore the master can use it as he pleases. There must be no interference on the part of the instrument.

16 I will betroth you to me in righteousness and in justice, in steadfast love, and in mercy. (Hos 2:19)

Love takes different forms in our lives and regards its object in many different ways. The love set forth in this passage is the highest and closest and most tender that human hearts can know, and it pictures to us a glory of affection between Christ's heart and ours, such as no words can adequately express. It is one of the latest revelations that come to a soul. At first we seek his *gifts* only, but at last we seek *him*. At first we are occupied with our needs and come to the Lord simply to have them supplied. But at last we lose sight of the gifts in our longing for the Giver and can be satisfied with nothing short of himself. Our souls cry out for a realized union with our Lord. And then there comes to us with untold joy the wonderful words, "As a bridegroom rejoices over his bride, so will your God rejoice over you," and we believe them and enter into our rest in the bosom of our Beloved!

17 *That they may all be one; even as thou, Father, art in me, and I in thee, that they also may be in us, so that the world may believe that thou hast sent me.* (Jn 17:21)

"That they may all be one!" It is all shut up in this phrase! One with the Father *as* the Son is one with him! Similarity of thought, of feeling, of desire, of love, of hate! We may have it all, if we will. We may walk through this life so united to Christ, that our cares and our interests, our sorrows and our joys, our purposes and our wishes will be the same. His will alone to govern, his mind alone to lead us. He in us, and we in him, will then be our life; until at last, so intermingled will our lives become, that we shall be able to say in truth, "Not I, but Christ." For self will vanish in such a union as this, and that great "I" of ours which so fills up our present horizon, will wilt down into nothing before the glory of his overcoming presence! *Be* one, then, since he says we are, and let the power of that oneness be lived out in every moment of your existence.

18 *But now the righteousness of God has been manifested apart from law, although the law and the prophets bear witness to it, the righteousness of God through faith in Jesus Christ for all who believe.* (Rom 3:21-22)

It is faith and faith only that can appropriate this righteousness that is ours in Christ. Just as we appropriate by faith the forgiveness that is ours in Christ, so must we appropriate by faith the patience that is ours in him, or the gentleness, or the meekness, or the longsuffering, or any other virtue we may need.

Our own efforts will not procure righteousness for us, any more than they will procure forgiveness. The Apostle Paul prays that he may be found in Christ, not having his own righteousness, which is of the law, but that which is through the faith of Christ, the righteousness which is of God by faith.

19 *Keep me as the apple of the eye; / hide me in the shadow of thy wings.* (Ps 17:8)

The mother hen keeps her little chickens under the shadow of her wings, and so will the Lord keep us, *if* we will let him. But this is a very large "if." What would we think of a little chicken which should stand off by itself, trembling with fright when danger was near, and saying, "I am not worthy to go under my mother's wing. I am too little, and too weak, and too insignificant. I must wait to go under until I am stronger and more worthy of her love"? Would not the mother hen have answered such a foolish little chicken by saying, "It is just because you *are* little and weak that I am spreading out my wings to cover you and am clucking for you to come. If you were grown large and strong, I would not want you. Your littleness and your weakness are your claim to my care."

20 *He will not let your foot be moved, / he who keeps you will not slumber. / Behold, he who keeps Israel / will neither slumber nor sleep. / The Lord is your keeper.* (Ps 121:3-5)

This psalm might be called the "Bible Keep." The Keep in an ancient castle was always the strongest and best protected room in the castle, the one which could be the last reached by any enemy. In this Keep all the sick and weak and helpless inmates of the castle were hidden in every time of danger. The qualification for entrance was simply and only need and weakness. How foolish then it would have been for any to have made their weakness the reason for remaining outside! And yet how continually is this done towards the Lord's Keep.

21 *I am sure that he is able to guard until that Day what has been entrusted to me.* (2 Tm 1:12)

If we know him, we can not fail to trust him. No one who knows him ever did. And this after all is the true secret of confidence—knowledge of the trustworthiness of the one to be trusted. We act on this in our earthly affairs and are never so silly as to look inside ourselves to see whether we can or ought to trust another. We look at that other instead, and try to find out his character and his ways. But in their intercourse with the Lord, many act on an entirely different principle. They look at themselves for a warrant and ground of trust, instead of at him. They behold self and its untrustworthiness and are filled with doubts and despair. Whereas a single soul-look at him will fill us with perfect peace, because of *his* utter trustworthiness.

22 *Have no anxiety about anything, but in everything by prayer and supplication with thanksgiving let your requests be made known to God.* (Phil 4:6)

We must give up all care of our own, by an utter surrender of everything to the Divine Caretaker, and by an implicit trust in him; and then we must just simply let him know our wants and our needs from day to day. If we do this honestly and persistently, the result will unfailingly be that the peace of God will keep our hearts and minds.

I remember once hearing of a man who thought he could not live unless he kept himself alive. He was afraid his breath would stop if he did not keep it going by his own efforts, and he tried so hard to keep breathing, that he nearly strangled himself in the struggle. His family in great alarm called in a physician, who, seeing at once the difficulty, called out to him peremptorily to stop trying to breathe. "I shall die if I do," gasped out the poor man. "Die then," exclaimed the doctor, "but STOP!" The man, overborne by the voice of authority, obeyed, and the moment he stopped trying to breathe, his breath came easily and without effort.

It is the same with some Christians. They are trying to keep themselves alive, and their life is nearly strangled in the effort. If they would but give up trying to live and would let Christ keep them alive, they would find themselves living easily and without effort.

23 *Rest in the Lord, and wait patiently for Him; / fret not thyself because of him who prospereth in his way, / because of the man who bringeth wicked devices to pass.*

(Ps 37:7, KJV)

The psalm speaks of "rest in the Lord," not in circumstances, or things, or people, and therefore this rest takes the "fret" out of life. Divine rest is to the soul what resting in a bed is to the body. We all know the delightful relaxation from every strain which comes to us in bed—the delicious letting go of the whole body in a perfect abandonment of ease and comfort. Such is the ease of soul that comes from resting "in the Lord." This rest implies perfect confidence in him.

If one should lie down in a bed that was in any way insecure, and was therefore liable to fall, it would be impossible to abandon oneself to rest. We would be compelled to hold on to something else, to keep ourselves safe in such a bed as that. It must be because Christians do not really believe the Lord alone to be a perfectly secure resting-place that they seek so eagerly for something else to hold on to: some good feelings, or good works, some church ordinances, or some special and remarkable experiences. What would we think of the foolishness of a man who was afraid his bed could not support him and tried to hold himself up by ropes attached to the ceiling? Yet this is nothing compared to the foolishness of those Christians who say they are resting in Christ and who yet are holding on to other supports.

24 *Therefore, while the promise of entering his rest remains, let us fear lest any of you be judged to have failed to reach it. For good news came to us just as to them; but* *the message which they heard did not benefit them, because it did not meet with faith in the hearers.* (Heb 4:1-2)

Notice the expressions "entering his rest." We cannot work for this rest, nor purchase it, nor provide it; we simply "enter into" the rest provided for us by one, who offers himself to us as our resting place. Just as we rest in a strong and loving earthly friend, who promises to help us through a difficulty, so must we rest in the Lord; and it requires faith on our part in both cases alike. If we doubt our friend, we cannot rest, no matter how much we may try; and if we doubt our Lord, we cannot rest either, no matter how much we may try. For rest comes always by trusting, not by trying.

25 *Take my yoke upon you, and learn from me; for I am gentle and lowly in heart, and you will find rest for your souls.* (Mt 11:29)

Surrender, faith, and obedience are necessary at every step of the divine progress, and nowhere more necessary than here. Without them, rest is simply impossible in the very nature of things. The little child rests in its mother, only when it yields unquestioning submission to her control and trusts implicitly in her love. The ox that yields to the yoke without chafing rests under it; while the young bullock, "unaccustomed to the yoke," finds it a galling burden. Truly many Christians have less sense than the dumb animals; for the animals, when they find the yoke inevitable, yield to it and it becomes easy, while we are tempted to chafe and worry under it as long as life lasts.

Learn to "take" the yoke upon you. Do not wait for it to be forced on you; but bow your neck to it willingly and "take" it. Say "Yes, Lord" to each expression of his will in all the circumstances of your life. Say it with full consent to everything, to the loss of your money, or the loss of your health, or to the malice of enemies, or the cruelty of friends. Take each yoke as it comes, and in the taking you will find rest.

26 *When He giveth quietness, who then can make trouble? (Jb 34:29, KJV)*

Among the peaks of the Sierra Nevada mountains, not far from the busy whirl of San Francisco, lies Lake Tahoe. It is twenty-three miles long, ten miles wide, and so deep that the line at 1,900 feet does not touch bottom; and it lies 5,000 feet above the neighboring ocean. Storms come and go in lower waters, but this lake is so still and its water so clear that the eye can penetrate, it is said, a hundred feet into its depths. A bell can be heard for ten or twenty miles. Around its mild verdant sides are the mountains, ever crowned with snow. The sky above is as calm as the motionless water. Nature loses scarcely anything of its clear outline as it is reflected there. Here the soul may learn something of what *rest* is, as day after day one opens one's heart to let the sweet influences of nature's sabbath enter and reign. And this is but a faint type of what we may find in Christ.

In the pressure of the greatest responsibilities, in the worry of the smallest cares, in the perplexity of life's moments of crisis, we may have the Lake Tahoe rest in the fastnesses of God's will. Learn to live in this rest; and in the calm of spirit that it will give, your soul will reflect as in a mirror the "beauty of the Lord," and the tumult of men's lives will be calmed in your presence as your tumults have been calmed in the presence of God.

27 *I appeal to you therefore, brethren, by the mercies of God, to present your bodies as a living sacrifice, holy and acceptable to God, which is your spiritual worship.*
(Rom 12:1)

However widely Christians may differ on other subjects, however divergent may be their views of truth or of doctrine, there is one point upon which every thoughtful soul will agree: and that is the fact that we all are called to an entire surrender of ourselves to the will of God. We are made for union with him, and the only pathway to this must of course be a perfect harmony between our will and his. For "how *can* two walk together except they be agreed?" Therefore God's commands to us to be holy are all based upon the fact that he to whom we belong is holy.

28 *Not every one who says to me, "Lord, Lord," shall enter the kingdom of heaven, but he who does the will of my Father who is in heaven.* (Mt 7:21)

God's purpose in our redemption was our entire consecration. Christians too often look upon consecration as something extra added on to salvation, not necessarily an essential part; and therefore think it is optional whether they enter into it or not, as they may please. However, the Bible declares that salvation is nothing, if it does not ultimately lead to holiness; for salvation in God's thought *is* holiness.

29 *Awaiting our blessed hope, the appearing of the glory of our great God and Savior Jesus Christ, who gave himself for us to redeem us from all iniquity and to purify for himself a people of his own who are zealous for good deeds.*
(Ti 2:13-14)

It is striking to notice that of the many announcements made concerning the work Christ came to accomplish, nearly every one declares it to be the deliverance from *sin*, rather than the escape of *punishment*. It is a salvation to *holiness*, rather than a salvation to *heaven*. Of course punishment is escaped and heaven is gained, in the nature of things, when we are saved from sin; since the greater always involves the less. But the vital thing in the redemption of Christ is evidently to redeem "from all iniquity," and "purify for himself a people of his own who are zealous for good deeds."

30 *Then I said, "Lo, I come; / in the roll of the book it is written of me; / I delight to do thy will, O my God; / thy law is within my heart."* (Ps 40:7-8)

Do we "delight" to do God's will? The enemy is always trying to get in the word duty instead of the word delight; he says a stern "you must" instead of the loving "you may." When a mother cares for her child from duty only, the tender sweetness of the mother love has gone. When the husband or wife begins to say only "I ought" instead of "I delight to" in relationship to the other, the home becomes a prison. There is no slavery like the slavery of love, but its chains are sweet. It knows nothing of "sacrifice," no matter what may be given up. It "delights to do the will" of the beloved one.

Our Lord can never be satisfied until this is the attitude of our souls towards him. His purposes of grace for us are that there should be harmony between our wills and his: not two wills crossing one another, but two wills made one. Has it become so with us that we delight to do his will? If not, the choice is before us now, and we must decide it.

31 *The Lord, the God of their fathers, sent persistently to them by his messengers, because he had compassion on his people and on his dwelling place; but they kept mocking the messengers of God ... till the wrath of the Lord rose against his people.* (2 Chr 36:15-16)

A watchful walk with the Lord would have saved Judah from it all. They had had warnings without number, through the whole course of their decline. In the same way, I feel sure that no soul now falls into backsliding or captivity, without continued and often-repeated warning, both from within and without. The Lord sends messengers to such now, just as he did to Judah then, because he has compassion on them: messengers of outward sorrow, and suffering, and loss, or messengers of inward condemnation and heaviness of heart. The Holy Spirit speaks to them in a voice they cannot mistake, giving them a sight of their condition and its dangers, and drawing them back to obedience tenderly and lovingly, or seeking to drive them with stern rebuke. We must take heed to every warning sent in love and compassion to save us from backsliding, even though it may be but the slight inward check or call of the indwelling Spirit.

November

1   *Arise, go over this Jordan, you and all this people, into the land which I am giving to them, to the people of Israel.*

(Jos 1:2)

The Book of Joshua opens on the children of Israel encamped in the plains of Moab "on this side Jordan, in the wilderness." Their long weary wanderings, since they had refused to enter the land forty years before, had not brought them any nearer Canaan than they were when they set out. They were on the borders then; they were only on the borders now. They had been moving, certainly, during all these forty years, but like a great deal of what is called "religious growth," their course had not been "upward and onward." They had gone round and round in that dreary wilderness, doubling on their track continually, and journeying onward, only to journey back again. Now a river lay between them and the land of their possession. Had they gone in at first, at Kadesh-barnea, they would have had only an unseen boundary to cross and the transition would not have been so strongly marked.

So I believe that in the experience of the Christian, there need not be that definite step, to which so many object, in entering into the more full enjoyment of the promises of the gospel, if only at our conversion we were taught that we were well able to overcome the land and were urged to go in at once and possess it. Doubtless some do thus enter in at Kadesh-barnea. But the majority of Christians, like the Israelites, fail to enter in at first, because of unbelief, and are turned back like them to wander in the wilderness described in chapter seven of Romans.

2 If thou dost kill this people as one man, then the nations who have heard thy fame will say, "Because the Lord was not able to bring this people into the land which he swore to give to them, therefore he has slain them in the wilderness."

(Nm 14:15-16)

God's object in redeeming his people out of Egypt had been to bring them into the promised land. "I have come down," he said in Exodus, "to deliver them out of the hand of the Egyptians, and to bring them up out of that land to"—what? the wilderness, to wander there forty years?—no—"to a good and broad land, a land flowing with milk and honey." Therefore, for the sake of his own glory, it was necessary that his people should go in and be planted in the land of their inheritance.

It is the same with us. We shall enter into possession of the promises, into that land of blessing and of rest which corresponds spiritually to the Canaan of the Israelites. It is not only a privilege God gives us but a command he utters: "Abide in me." "Be filled with the Spirit." "Reckon yourselves to be dead indeed to sin." "Be careful for nothing." "Let not your heart be troubled, neither let it be afraid." All these are glorious privileges, but they are also positive commands. Unless we enter into this blessed fullness of salvation, we will surely give occasion to the world to say that God is not able to bring us into the land which he promised us.

3   *Have I not commanded you! Be strong and of good courage; be not frightened, neither be dismayed; for the Lord your God is with you wherever you go.* (Jos 1:9)

The Lord commands us to go in and possess the land of our inheritance. God's commands are even more comforting than his promises; for if he commands me to do a thing, I am sure he will give me the power of his Spirit to do it. His commands are not grievous, we are told, but surely they would be grievous, if we were utterly unable to obey them. It would have been a grievous thing indeed had he commanded the children of Israel to go in and possess the land of Canaan, knowing that they were utterly unable to do it, had he not himself intended to supply them with the power. In fact, he uses his very command as the reason why they should have no fear. "Have not I commanded you?" he asks. He tells us that we need have no fear in doing what he has commanded us to do, for he is in every command he gives and will always bestow the necessary power to obey it.

4   *Every place that the sole of your foot will tread upon I have given to you, as I promised to Moses.* (Jos 1:3)

Notice that the Lord says "I *have* given," not "I *will* give." It was all theirs in the purpose and mind of God, but unless the chosen people actually *went* and set their feet upon it, it did not become theirs practically and experimentally. This is necessarily true of any gift. The giver may give it with all the sincerity and goodwill possible, but it never really comes into the recipient's possession until he actually receives it, and appropriates it, and calls it his own. Even though a gift should be laid on the table, or put into the pocket of a friend, he will not possess it unless he closes his hand of acceptance over it and says mentally, "it is mine."

5   *I know that the Lord has given you the land, and that the fear of you has fallen upon us, and that all the inhabitants of the land melt away before you.* (Jos 2:9)

The harlot Rahab of Jericho is a wonderful example of how acceptable faith is to the Lord, even when exercised in the midst of great ignorance and distance from himself. Her faith so strengthened the faith of the spies that they returned to Joshua with the triumphant news, "Truly the Lord has given all the land into our hands; and moreover all the inhabitants of the land are fainthearted because of us." How different the report of these spies from that of the spies sent out forty years before. The giants were as mighty now as then, and the cities as great, and they themselves were as weak. But then they had left out the Lord and had measured their enemies with themselves; and now Rahab had brought him in by saying, "I know that *the Lord* has given you the land." When God is brought into the scene and our enemies are measured with him, there can no longer be any doubt or fear remaining. I believe that if we could send out spies into the land of our possession, as Israel did, we would also find that our enemy faints because of us, and that he knows, whether we do or not, that the Lord has delivered all the land into our hands. He is an already-conquered foe, and the courage of faith will soon discover this, let him bluster as he may.

6 *When those who bore the ark had come to the Jordan, and the feet of the priests bearing the ark were dipped in the brink of the water . . . the waters coming down from above stood and rose up in a heap far off. (Jos 3:15-16)*

It required a far stronger faith to cross the Jordan than to cross the Red Sea; and the faith which can trust for the forgiveness of sins needs to be greatly strengthened, in order to believe in victory over sin. To me, this stepping into a brimming river, when as yet there was no sign of a path, is one of the grandest pictures of faith on record. I can fancy the heathen nations around, if they witnessed the scene, sneering at the folly and presumption of a people who could act thus. They must have known only too well that they could not trust their gods to part the river. But I think their cry afterwards must have been,

"Surely no people have a god like these people!" Could the world but see more of this sublime sort of faith among Christians now, I feel sure they would be won to yield allegiance to a God who can thus be trusted and who never fails his people's confidence.

7 How can we who died to sin still live in it? Do you not know that all of us who have been baptized into Christ Jesus were baptized into his death? (Rom 6:2-3)

In experience this is an intensely practical thing. For nothing so gives victory over sin as to reckon one's self to be *dead* to it, and nothing so enables the soul to walk in righteousness as to realize its resurrection life in Christ. It may be difficult to explain this theologically or doctrinally; but to my mind the great point in studying the Bible is to get at its truths experimentally; and thousands of witnesses can testify to the blessed reality of being dead to sin and alive to God in Jesus Christ. I have known lifelong sins conquered in this way, that had not yielded one iota to all the struggles and efforts of years. I knew a lady with such an irritable temper that she was almost intolerable to live with. She was a Christian, and she grieved over it with bitter sorrow, but seemed to find it impossible to get the victory by years of struggling and agonizing. Finally, when she was almost in despair, she was told by someone to reckon herself dead to sin. If she did, God would make it real by the power of his Spirit. In her despair she grasped at the hope, and kneeling before her open Bible, with her finger on Romans 6:2, she dared to obey the divine command and reckoned herself, on the authority of God's own word, to be dead indeed to sin, but alive to God through Jesus Christ. It seemed like taking a step off a fearful precipice into a sheer abyss. But, as always, the step of faith found the rock beneath, and according to her faith it was done to her. She met every temptation to irritability by saying, "I am dead to sin. I am crucified with Christ. I am alive in him." From that hour, now many years ago, not even an inward ruffle has disturbed her peace.

8 *Whatever you ask in prayer, believe that you have received it, and it will be yours.* (Mk 11:24)

I believe that the Christian is called to shout the shout of victory even at the very moment when his foes seem stronger than ever. I mean just this, that if we meet our enemy as an already-conquered foe and claim by faith our victory over him in Christ, we shall overcome far more quickly, than if we look upon him as an enemy who has yet to be conquered by our vigorous conflict against him. "This is the victory that overcomes the world, our faith" (1 Jn 5:4). I have found that the little words, "Jesus saves me, Jesus saves me *now*," repeated over and over in any great stress of temptation will bring a far speedier victory than I can gain in any other way. For our Lord himself says, "Whoever says to this mountain, 'Be taken up and cast into the sea,' and does not doubt in his heart, but believes that what he says will come to pass, it will be done for him" (Mk 11:23).

9 *As smoke is driven away, so drive them away; / as wax melts before fire.* (Ps 68:2)

The Lord commands us to drive out every enemy from our hearts and lives. If we refuse to utterly drive them out and seek merely to make them tributary to us, we shall find ourselves continually enslaved and oppressed by those very enemies whom we have allowed to remain. The Lord promises to deliver us from the hands of all our enemies and to enable us always to triumph. But if we refuse, as the Israelites did, to avail ourselves fully of this promised strength, we shall suffer the same results. This accounts for the condition of so many Christians, who find themselves enslaved and oppressed continually by their inward enemies and whose victories, even when they cry to the Lord and are victorious, are yet followed by ever-recurring defeats. They groan under it and cannot understand it. But the problem lies in this, that they have not utterly driven out their enemies. They have thought perhaps that they could not. They may have said, "My circumstances are so peculiar, or my temperament is so sensitive, or my temptations are so great" that they have excused themselves. They have not even *expected* to be entirely delivered from their irritable tempers, or their roots of bitterness, or their seasons of discouragement, or their sharp tongues, but have felt themselves very successful if they have been able to make these things tributary, as it were, and have managed to keep them under by constant watchfulness and prayer. They compromise with the enemy, instead of utterly driving him out. In this way many Christians compromise with doubt, or with the disobedience of timidity, or with anxiety, or with a hundred other forms of evil, against which God's commands of utter renunciation and death have plainly gone forth. As a consequence, *he* no longer drives out the enemies *we* have allowed to remain, and they are indeed snares and traps for us, and scourges in our sides, and thorns in our eyes.

10

He who loves his life loses it, and he who hates his life in this world will keep it for eternal life. (Jn 12:25)

He alone who reckons himself dead, not simply to a few of his sins, but to every sin, can gain the continual victories and live the life of uniform triumph. I think it is just in this that the great difference arises in the experiences of those who enter into the land of promise now. With some, self seems to be swallowed up at once by the revelation of Christ and to lift up its head no more; while with others the death of self is accomplished only by slow degrees and through great conflicts. Through death to life is always God's way, and there is no other. If we would live, we must first die. We must lose our own life, if we would find the life that is hid with Christ in God. We must reckon ourselves dead before we can reckon ourselves to be alive. The more thorough and wide-reaching is the death, the more all-pervading and victorious will be the life. Is it not a grand proposal of the gospel, then, that we should put off at once and always the old man and put on forever the new man? And shall we hesitate to do it?

11 The people of Israel did what was evil in the sight of the Lord, forgetting the Lord their God, and serving the Baals and the Asheroth. (Jgs 3:7)

This sin of idolatry is very much misunderstood. Many Christians think it means only loving some human being too much, or being too fond of some earthly comfort or pleasure. But to my mind, idolatry is a far graver sin. Among the Israelites it meant worshipping a false god, and it means the same now among Christians. It matters little whether this god is one carved out of wood or stone, or carved out of our own imagination. If our thought or idea of God is different from the Lord whom the Bible reveals, we are really worshipping an idol. Understood in this sense, idolatry is a far more common sin today than we have tended to think.

Let me illustrate. How many people say to their children all through their childhood, "God does not love naughty children"? Nothing more directly contrary to the Bible or more untrue of the God of the Bible could be taught; for there we are told that "God so *loved* the world that he gave his only begotten Son" to die for it. To teach innocent little children such a sad untruth as this is to set up an idol for them to worship. When they grow older and are compelled to learn that the God of the Bible is much different than the god they have learned about, that he hates only the sin but loves the sinner, is it to be wondered at that they are so wedded to their false idea of him that they find it very difficult to believe that he can really be what the Bible declares him to be? My heart aches at the thought of the idols being fashioned in the hearts of so many young children at this very day. I believe that many people have been so burdened by such false ideas of God that they are never able in this life to shake off the doubts and discouragements they have caused. I am convinced that the amount of this sort of idolatry in the church today would be appalling, if we could but see it in all its magnitude and deformity.

12 Israel served the Lord all the days of Joshua, and all the days of the elders who outlived Joshua and had known all the work which the Lord did for Israel. (Jos 24:31)

The children of Israel served the true God as long as any were alive who remembered the wonderful deliverance out of Egypt. But when Joshua died and all the elders that outlived Joshua, who had seen all the great works of the Lord, then they soon forgot him and served other gods. I think this is an example of one form of idolatry which may be peculiar to the higher stages of Christian experience. The soul, becoming absorbed in the deeper truths of our religion, is apt to lose sight of the fundamental doctrine of coming out of Egypt, or of justification by faith, and to speak and to think so exclusively of the fruits of the Spirit and the life and walk of the believer, as almost to forget the necessity of pressing the foundational truths of salvation, and the way of entrance into the spiritual life. This leads to a one-sided statement of truth that may become very dangerous, especially to the soul which has had no clear teaching on the other side, and may end in very false views of God. May the lessons of warning contained in our book save us from such mistakes.

13 Barak said to her [Deborah], "If you will go with me, I will go; but if you will not go with me, I will not go." (Jgs 4:8)

Deborah sets forth most strikingly the lesson of God's strength made perfect in our weakness. A woman here leads the armies of the Lord against a captain who had nine hundred chariots of iron and who for twenty years mightily oppressed the children of Israel. Even Barak, whose name means "thunder," the strong captain in Israel, dared not go without her. This is a picture, it seems to me, of Paul's teaching in 2 Corinthians 12:7-10: "When I am weak then I am strong." It is a striking illustration of the truth that God has chosen the weak things of the world to confound the mighty that no flesh might glory in his presence. For Deborah said to Barak, "I will surely go with you; nevertheless, the road on which you are going will not lead to your glory, for the Lord will sell Sisera into the hand of a woman."

14 *As obedient children, do not be conformed to the passions of your former ignorance.* (1 Pt 1:14)

No position in grace, no height of Christian attainment can keep the soul from failing. Only the present power of an indwelling Holy Spirit can do this, and nothing but continual faithfulness to the Lord can secure his abiding presence. We never, at any stage of our experience, reach a place where we may relax in our obedience or become indifferent in our trust. Obedience must keep pace with knowledge, and our trust must be daily and hourly fixed on our Savior, or all will go wrong. Sanctification is not a state so much as a walk, and every moment of that walk we need the Spirit's power and the Spirit's presence as much as we did at first. Not even after dwelling in the land of promise for many years are we strong enough to do without this. Always, from the beginning to the end of our Christian life, obedience and trust are the two essential conditions of our triumph. We must make no more compromise with evil at the end than at the beginning. If failure comes, it will always arise from one or the other of these two causes: either want of consecration or want of trust. It is never the strength of our enemies, nor our own weakness that causes us to fall. While the Lord continues to be with us, no man can stand before us all the days of our life; and if we will only steadfastly abide in him, we need not be in the least discouraged at the thought of the temptations that surround us on every hand.

15 *Then Boaz said to Ruth, "Now, listen, my daughter, do not go to glean in another field or leave this one, but keep close to my maidens."* (Ru 2:8)

Those who turn their backs on the world to seek the Lord, even though very ignorant of all the blessings in store for them, find themselves soon gleaning in the field of Christ, who is our near kinsman, and who, as Boaz did, causes his servants to leave behind grain for us to glean. Ruth had come to trust under the wings of the God of Israel; and no one ever yet trusted in him and was confounded.

This it seems to me is the first experience of the returning sinner. Figuratively speaking, he leaves his father and his mother and the land of his nativity, as Ruth did, and comes to a people he has not known before. Then he begins to glean and gathers in from the Lord's harvest fields spiritual food to supply his daily needs. For a while, the soul is satisfied with this.

But a time comes when a deeper want is felt. "Naomi her mother-in-law said to her, 'My daughter, should I not seek a home for you that it may be well with you?'" Naomi knew that Ruth needed a married life, a home, and a care-taker, and all the joys of wedded union. In a similar way, the soul of the believer begins sooner or later to hunger and thirst after this rest in a realized union with Christ, of which the marriage union is so precious a type.

16 *She answered, "I am Ruth, your maidservant; spread your skirt over your maidservant, for you are next of kin." And he [Boaz] said, "May you be blessed by the Lord, my daughter; you have made this last kindness greater than the first." (Ru 3:9-10)*

Ruth's claim looked like presumption, but Boaz called it "kindness." Our Lord, too, delights in every claim we make upon him for this realized oneness with himself, however bold it may seem to us. It is indeed his own prayer for us, "That they all may be one; as thou Father art in me, and I in thee, that they also may be one in us: that the world may believe that thou hast sent me." Far dearer to him than the greatest activities of service, is the longing of the heart to know this oneness and the claim of faith that comes boldly to his feet to receive it.

17 *Be still, and know that I am God.* (Ps 46:10)

I cannot but feel that we need more of this "being still" in our Christian experience. There is too much restless anxiety about our prayers, too much the feeling that unless we wrestle and agonize over things, they will not turn out well. I witnessed an illustration of this not long ago. I was visiting a mother whose little boy was playing in the room. We were talking about prayer and asking each other what sort of praying was right—the trusting kind, or the agonizing kind. Suddenly we were interrupted by the child, who asked for a cookie. His mother said yes at once and went to the cupboard for them, but found the cookie jar empty. She explained things to the child, but said she would send his older sister for some. The child saw his sister go out. A good child would have gone on playing again, and would have waited quietly and trustingly until the girl returned. But this child stood at his mother's elbow, saying over and over, "Mother, give me a cookie. I want a cookie. Please, let me have a cookie!" Finally, our conversation was drowned in the noise of his wailing, and we could do nothing but sit still in the best patience we could muster.

My question about prayer was answered. Since then, I have never dared agonize over any request I have made to the Lord. I do not mean, however, that we are to forget our prayers or be indifferent about their results, but simply that, having made our request known, we must then wait in quiet and patient faith, sure that our Lord will not rest until he has finished the matter we have put into his hands. We are not always prepared ourselves to receive an immediate answer to our prayers. We do not give the best things in our possession to our youngest children, even though they ask, lest they should hurt themselves, or spoil the things. We wait until they grow old enough to take the proper care of them and to understand their use. Our Father is too wise to give us what we are not yet prepared to receive. But when we ask him, he will first make us ready for the gift, and will then bestow it when we can receive and use it.

18 *That they may all be one; even as thou, Father, art in me, and I in thee, that they also may be in us.* (Jn 17:21)

Seek after this oneness with all your heart. Your Lord intends it for you and will grant it, as soon as he has prepared your soul to enter into it. Let nothing discourage you. Though he tarry, wait for him, for he will surely come; and if you will but persevere, the blessed day must and will come, sooner or later, when your soul shall be satisfied with the fullness of his love, and you shall abide continually in his conscious presence. He will come and take up his abode with you, and, like Ruth, you shall "find rest" at last in the heart of your Heavenly Bridegroom.

19 *If you keep my commandments, you will abide in my love, just as I have kept my Father's commandments and abide in his love.* (Jn 15:10)

There are but few joys like the joy of entire surrender to the Lord Jesus Christ. The soul that has tried it knows this, and to the soul that has not, I can only say that the control of unselfish love is always lovely, even when that love is earthly, because in the nature of things love *can* choose only the best for its beloved one and *must* pour out itself to the last drop to help and to bless that one. Therefore, the control of God, who is love, who is not merely loving, but is Love itself, must be and can be nothing but infinite and fathomless blessing.

20 *David inquired of the Lord, "Shall I go and attack these Philistines?" And the Lord said to David, "Go and attack the Philistines and save Keilah."* (1 Sm 23:2)

It appears that David led his people on to continuous victory. The secret of it was his childlike dependence upon the Lord. Every step of the way he testified continually to his own weakness and to God's strength. Over and over we have the expression used concerning him, "and the Lord was with him."

When confronted with the giant Goliath, he said to Saul, who told him he was not able to fight the Philistine, "The Lord who delivered me from the paw of the lion and from the paw of the bear, will deliver me from the hand of this Philistine." In everything, David saw that God was present in the situation. Unlike Saul, of whom it was said that he "inquired not of the Lord," we find David continually, in every time of need, going to the Lord for advice and guidance. And the Lord always answered these inquiries as simply as they were asked. The simplicity and directness of this intercourse and communion between David and the Lord his God is very striking and reveals a most blessed oneness. In a faint way it prefigures the human life of dependence and obedience of our Lord Jesus Christ and teaches us our own privileges of a direct and personal intercourse with our Father, who has told us "in everything to make our requests known to him"; and who surely must mean to grant us as sure a response as he did to David. Let us then in everything "inquire of the Lord" with childlike confidence, believing that he hears us and will certainly reply.

21 *He has delivered the inhabitants of the land into my hand; and the land is subdued before the Lord and his people.* (1 Chr 22:18)

The kingdom of David is a type of that stage in the soul's history, when only conflict is known, and when Christ is apprehended only in his character as our conquering Captain, leading us on to battle. Many souls know no other Christian life but this and live therefore in perpetual conflict. But David's battles were for the purpose of conquering Israel's enemies. When he had accomplished this purpose, he handed over into Solomon's control a kingdom which had "rest from its enemies." Christ as our Captain also meets and conquers our enemies for us, in order that he may hand over the inward kingdom, thus made peaceful and at rest. Never to pass beyond the experience of conflict into the experience of peace would seem to prove that the soul had not apprehended Christ as a victorious Captain, before whom the land should be subdued, and into whose hand all its enemies should be delivered. Many Christians stumble here and never pass beyond the reign of David. They cannot believe in the accomplished victories of our Lord Jesus Christ but think they must fight and conquer the foe for themselves. They lift up, not the shield of *faith*, but the shield of *doubt* and are consequently smitten by the fiery darts of the enemy. We must know the Lord Jesus Christ as our conquering King and Captain, so that we will put all our battles into his hand to fight and leave all our enemies to him to vanquish. He has overcome the world by actual conflict. We overcome by faith (1 Jn 5:4). The fiery darts of the enemy spent their strength on him. He has furnished us with a shield of faith with which we can quench them all (Eph 6:16). By faith we can say in truth, "The land is subdued before the Lord and before his people," and can enter into the kingdom of rest and peace, which he has obtained for us.

22 *When the queen of Sheba had seen all the wisdom of Solomon ... She said to the king ... "Your wisdom and prosperity surpass the report which I heard." (1 Kgs 10:4, 6-7)*

The whole world was attracted by the report of the riches and glory of Solomon's kingdom, and the Queen of Sheba came from her far country to Jerusalem to see if all that had been told her could indeed be true. In the same way, we may be sure the world will be attracted by the report of Christian lives that are filled with spiritual riches and power and wisdom, and will gather from far and near to see if the story they have heard can indeed be a true one. When they have seen it and have witnessed the peace in the midst of trial, and the inward joy overpowering the outward sorrow, and the victory over temptation, and the overflowing wealth of grace, they will be forced to acknowledge that it is indeed true, that "no eye has seen, nor ear heard, / nor the heart of man conceived, / what God has prepared for those who love him." Thus the saying of our Lord in the Sermon on the Mount will be fulfilled, that our light shall so "shine before men," that they, seeing our good works, may "glorify," not us, but "our Father who is in heaven."

23 *Peace I leave with you; my peace I give to you; not as the world gives do I give to you. Let not your hearts be troubled, neither let them be afraid. (Jn 14:27)*

Is the outside world so attracted by the report of your riches and spiritual power, that it asks you about your secret? Do your children see in you such patience that they are won over to love and serve your God? Do your friends have cause to know from the outward peace of your daily life, that the God of peace reigns within, and are their hearts attracted to his service?

Alas! I am afraid that the reverse is too often the case and that one great cause of the small number of conversions in a church or a community is to be found in the poor and meager sort of Christianity that exists there. How can a husband think it desirable to be a Christian when he sees his wife with a sort of Christianity that seems only to make her uncomfortable and gloomy; or how can children be attracted to a religion which is professed by a cross or unreasonable father?

Once an unbeliever said something to me that I have never forgotten. We were talking together about Christianity, and I was urging its claims upon him, when he said, with marked emphasis and yet sadness, "If you Christians want the outside world to believe in your religion, you must have a better kind. Most of you seem to carry your religion as a man carries a headache. He does not want to get rid of his head, but he is forced to confess that it causes him a great deal of discomfort and suffering. You would not I suppose want to give up your religion, but you must acknowledge it often makes you mightily uncomfortable." Let us, then, seek to realize in our own individual experience all the fullness of our glorious salvation, that we may attract the world around us, by the beauty and blessedness of our lives, so that they may taste and see that the Lord *is* good and that he does indeed fulfill his promises.

24 *May you be strengthened with all power, according to his glorious might, for all endurance and patience with joy.* (Col 1:11)

We have need of patience with ourselves and with others: with those below and those above us, and with our equals: with those who love us and those who love us not: for the greatest things and the least: against sudden inroads of trouble and under our daily burden: disappointments as to the weather or the breaking of the heart: in the weariness of body or mind: in everyday wants or in the aching of sickness or the decay of age: in disappointment, losses, bereavement, injuries, reproaches: in heaviness of the heart, or its sickness amid delayed hopes.

The family is full of opportunities for the practice of this virtue, for we may be called upon at any moment for the almost heroic exercise of good temper and self-sacrifice. Parents must have patience with their children—patience with their tempers, patience with their understandings, patience with their progress. In all these things, from childhood's little troubles to the martyr's sufferings, we shall be ready to acknowledge that the one who has attained patience is master of himself.

25 *Open to me, my sister, my love, / my dove, my perfect one.* (Sg 5:2)

The Lord has always sought for a dwelling place in his people's midst. He loves them with such a yearning love, that he cannot keep away from them; and at almost the very first moment of Israel's deliverance out of Egypt, his word came to Moses, saying, "Let them make me a sanctuary, that I may dwell among them." They had not asked him to come, but he asked them to let him. He wanted a home among them. He might have made this home for himself by coming in power and taking forcible possession of one of their tents. But this would not have satisfied the love that wanted to be a welcomed guest. Similarly, he will not take forcible possession of any heart now, but knocks for admittance. "Open to me," he says to each one of us.

26 *You shall receive the gift of the Holy Spirit. For the promise is to you and to your children and to all that are far off, every one whom the Lord our God calls to him.*
(Acts 2:38-39)

This promise is surely intended for you, for, without it, the Christian life is but poor and dwarfed. Do not be satisfied without it for even so much as another day. The steps to reach it are very simple. First, convince yourself from the scriptures that the baptism of the Spirit is a gift intended for you. Then come to the Lord in simple faith to ask for it. Having put your case into his hands, leave it there in childlike trust, knowing that he will attend to your request, and that he is even more willing to give you the Holy Spirit than parents are to give good gifts to their children.

Take 1 John 5:14 and act on it: "This is the confidence which we have in him, that if we ask anything according to his will he hears us." You are asking for that which is according to his will, therefore, you know that he hears you, and knowing this, you must know still more, and must believe that you have the petitions you desired of him. By faith, claim it as your present possession. Begin to praise him for his wondrous gift. And it will come to pass, just as it did to Israel, that "the glory of the Lord will fill the house of the Lord," and your hungry soul will be filled and satisfied with his presence.

27 *No one can serve two masters; . . . You cannot serve God and mammon.* (Mt 6:24)

The latter part of Solomon's reign and the divided rule which followed seem to me typical of the special dangers that are likely to beset the Christian at a later stage in the journey. No height of spiritual blessing or spiritual power can for a moment absolve us from the need for obedience and watchfulness. The temptation to antinomianism has often overwhelmed the church or the individual after seasons of peculiar blessing, and it needs to be especially guarded against. We can never forsake the written law of the Lord with impunity, no matter how advanced our spiritual life may be. We need to watch, lest, when seated in heavenly places in Christ, we should feel so far lifted above the usual temptations of life, that we are tempted to be less careful of our steps, that we walk continually in the law of our God.

28 *All the vessels of the house of God, great and small, and the treasures of the house of the Lord, and the treasures of the king and of his princes, all these he brought to Babylon.*
(2 Chr 36:18)

Babylon was not Egypt. Egypt, I believe, is a type of the state of nature out of which the church is brought, while Babylon is the state of worldliness and corruption into which unfaithfulness brings her. Babylon seems to be always used in scripture to set forth Satan's counterfeit of that which the Lord has made. If the Lord provides any good thing for his children, Satan provides a counterfeit of it, transforming himself even into an angel of light, if only he may deceive the elect. We do not hear of Babylon while Israel was in Egypt, nor during the early freshness of their joy in escaping from Egypt. Babylon was an enemy who came to light only in the advanced period of Israel's history. The church knew nothing of the danger which Babylon typifies during the early years of its existence, nor are Christians assailed by it right after their conversion. It is only when churches or individual believers have been drawn away from their faithful allegiance to the law of the Lord, when they have substituted the commandments and traditions of men for the commandments of God, and have begun to "mock the true messengers of the Lord, and despise his words and misuse his prophets," that the danger comes in. A false and corrupt rule takes possession of the heart and carries it captive. The precious truths, which were part of the worship of the true God typified by the "vessels of the house of God," are taken for the service of the false religion.

29 *Since all these things are thus to be dissolved, what sort of persons ought you to be in lives of holiness and godliness, waiting for and hastening the coming of the day of God. (2 Pt 3:11-12)*

I am well aware that this is a subject which does not interest all Christians and which is considered fanciful and unprofitable by many. But consider what the angel declared to the disciples on the Mount of Olives, while they looked toward the heavens where a cloud had just received their Lord out of their sight: "This Jesus, who was taken up from you into heaven, will come in the same way as you saw him go into heaven." It must certainly be important for us to know it, and to enter into the mind of God about it. I believe myself that there is hardly any truth which has so great an effect in making Christians unworldly as this.

If we expect one who is absent from us to return at any moment, we shall surely make ourselves ready for his coming and will take care to arrange matters so that when he comes he shall not find us engaged in anything of which we think he will not approve. It is striking to notice that the Lord's exhortations to holiness of life are always based, not on the fear of death, but on the hope of his return and its unexpectedness.

30 *Blessed are those servants whom the master finds awake when he comes. . . . You also must be ready; for the Son of man is coming at an unexpected hour. (Lk 12:37, 40)*

I am convinced that such passages as this teach us that the thought of the unexpectedness of our Lord's return is a far more powerful incentive to holiness than the thought of death; and I believe the church has suffered great loss from having overlooked this. It all depends upon how much we love him, whether we are longing to see him back. Our present walk and life will surely be greatly changed by a firm belief on our part that at any moment we may see him and hear the voice of the trumpet that calls us to his side. Let us ask ourselves a few solemn questions here. Are we, like the early Christians, waiting for him to come? Are we *ready* for his coming? We cannot wait until we are ready. What would we think of a housekeeper, who was expecting a visit from a very distinguished guest, and whose house should be turned upside down with repairs, and painting, and cleaning, but who would say to us, "Oh, yes, I am waiting longingly for my friend to arrive, and am expecting him at any moment"? I am sure we would be amazed by such waiting as that and would say, "But how can you wait for him until you are ready? Wouldn't his coming be very inconvenient and ill-timed? Wouldn't you prefer that he delay his coming, until you have prepared a comfortable place in which to receive him?"

We may well pause and think, therefore, whether *we* are ready for our Lord's coming. Are our houses, and our lives, and our churches prepared to receive him? Would his coming just at this present moment seem inconvenient or ill-timed to us? If we knew that he were coming next week, would we go on with our lives as they are and carry out our present plans and purposes for our few remaining days?

I remember being impressed by John Wesley's reply to a friend who asked him how he would spend the day if he knew he were to die that night. After a solemn pause, Wesley replied, "I should do just the things I have already planned to do. I should attend to the business I have laid out. I should see the friends I have expected to see. I should go to the places I have arranged for. I should read the books I have prepared. I should eat my meals, and take my usual rest, and should quietly await the hour of my death without one anxious thought." How wonderful to be so ready. Our Lord says to us, "You also must be ready; for the Son of man is coming at an unexpected hour."

December

1

Whoever is among you of all his people, may his God be with him, and let him go up to Jerusalem, which is in Judah, and rebuild the house of the Lord, the God of Israel.

(Ezr 1:3)

In Ezra we have the rebuilding of the temple, and in Nehemiah the walls of the city are rebuilt. The inward restoration must come first. The building of the temple in the first place, seems to me to be a type of the soul consciously surrendering itself to be the temple of the Holy Spirit. The rebuilding of this temple, typifies, I think, the restoration of the soul from backsliding or wandering, and a fresh surrender of the heart to the Lord, to be possessed and indwelt by him. It is what is happening, I believe, in many instances in the present day. Believers are being brought to a sense of their distance from the Lord, and are groaning under their captivity to their enemies. The song has issued from their hearts in the language used by the exiled Israelites to describe their own sad condition: "By the waters of Babylon, / there we sat down and wept, / when we remembered Zion" (Ps 137:1). These Christians have heard, as plainly as Israel of old, the call to go up to Jerusalem to build the house of the Lord and have obeyed this call. To such, this book of Ezra will be full of wonderful teaching.

2 *Now these were the people of the province who came up out of the captivity.... The whole assembly together was forty-two thousand three hundred and sixty.* (Ezr 2:1, 64)

Sometimes we have been inclined to wonder why there should occur now and then in the Bible these long lists of names. But if we think of them as sample pages out of the divine book of records, they assume a deep and precious interest. Just so, doubtless, is our Father keeping record of those now, who, in these days of half-heartedness and degeneracy, are offering themselves to him in glad surrender, to be his temple, and to be filled with his abiding presence!

3 *Make confession to the Lord the God of your fathers, and do his will; separate yourselves from the peoples of the land and from the foreign wives.* (Ezr 10:11)

To be holy involves being set apart for God, to be separated from everything that is evil. Therefore, when the soul has surrendered itself to the Lord to be his dwelling place, the searching power of his Holy Spirit begins to reveal the evil and calls for an entire separation from it.

This matter of the "foreign wives" seems to me to be a type of that wandering of the heart from the Lord, which is called "setting our affections on earthly things." The New Testament speaks of it as the "friendship of the world," and in James 4:4, we are told that this friendship is "enmity with God." The life of separation to the Lord must be real. Everything that could be considered union with "foreign wives" must be put away. The Lord must have our whole hearts, for our love is precious to him, and anything which entices our hearts from our allegiance to him must be given up. "He that loves father or mother more than me is not worthy of me; and he that loves son or daughter more than me is not worthy of me."

4 *Looking to Jesus the pioneer and perfecter of our faith.* (Heb 12:2)

It is a simple fact that we see what we look at and cannot see what we look away from. We cannot look to Jesus while we are looking at ourselves. The power for victory and the power for endurance are to come from looking to Jesus and considering him, not from looking to or considering ourselves, our circumstances, our sins, or our temptation. All looking at ourselves causes weakness and defeat. The reason for this is that when we look at ourselves, we see nothing but ourselves, and our own weakness, and poverty, and sin; and we do not, and cannot, see the remedy and the supply for these, and as a matter of course we are defeated. The remedy and the supply are there all the time, but they are not to be found in the place we are looking, for they are not in self, but in Christ; and we cannot be looking at ourselves and looking at Christ at the same time. It is a simple question of choice for us, whether it shall be *I* or *Christ*; whether we shall turn our backs on Christ and look at ourselves, or whether we shall turn our backs on self and look at Christ.

5 *You see the trouble we are in, how Jerusalem lies in ruins with its gates burned. Come, let us build the wall of Jerusalem.* (Neh 2:17)

Ezra describes how the temple was rebuilt and God's dwelling place restored. Now, Nehemiah raises the call to build up the wall of Jerusalem. Inward restoration always paves the way and prepares the heart for outward restoration; and this rebuilding of the walls of Jerusalem seems to me to typify the outward work and service of the Christian in whose heart the Lord dwells. Jerusalem may be taken as a figure of the church, and the building of her walls and gates, as symbolizing that building up of the church now, of which the Apostle speaks when he says, "So with yourselves; since you are eager for manifestations of the Spirit, strive to excel in building up the church" (1 Cor 14:12). "And his gifts were that some should be apostles, some prophets, some evangelists, some pastors and teachers, to equip the saints for the work of ministry, for building up the body of Christ" (Eph 4:11-12).

6 *And Joiada the son of Paseah and Meshullam the son of Besodeiah repaired the Old Gate; they laid its beams and set its doors, its bolts and its bars.* (Neh 3:6)

In chapter 3 of Nehemiah, we have a detailed account of the work that was done to the walls of Jerusalem and the names of the men who did it. This is a sample page out of the Lord's book of records. How precious to see God taking note of each man and of all the details of each man's work. Men may pass over lightly the work which their brethren do for the Lord, and may even think their own work not worth remembering; but the Lord never forgets the smallest thing. How little did Joiada the son of Paseah and Meshullam the son of Besodeiah think, as they laid the beams of the old gate and set the door amid the sneers and assaults of their enemies, that the record of their work was to go down to untold millions. The weakest laborer may be sure that he is honorably mentioned in that blessed book of records, which is kept in the Lord's own house on high.

7 *Fight the good fight of the faith; take hold of the eternal life to which you were called.* (1 Tm 6:12)

I am aware that those who teach a life of perfect rest and peace are sometimes supposed to mean that there are no more assaults from our enemy in such a life. But this is so manifestly a misunderstanding, that it hardly seems necessary to say anything about it. Yet it is so difficult to explain just what we do mean, that I do not wonder we are misunderstood. For it is one of those marvelous paradoxes in which two apparently irreconcilable things exist at the same moment and perfectly harmonize. Peace and war, rest and labor—they are one here. We fight, but it is the fight of faith, not of effort, for "our God fights for us," and therefore we are at perfect peace. We work, but it is not we who work, but God who works in us and through us, and therefore we rest. But to understand this, we must experience it. We work as the instrument works in the hand of the skillful workman. We fight as the baby fights, who hides its head in its mother's bosom.

8   *Thus I cleansed them from everything foreign, and I established the duties of the priest and Levites, each in his work.* (Neh 13:30)

Thus ends the book of Nehemiah. As Nehemiah dealt with the Israelites, cleansing them from everything foreign, so will the blessed Holy Spirit deal now in faithful and loving rebuke with every soul that returns afresh to the law of the Lord. What comfort this is! You may have wandered far from the Lord and have been taken captive by cruel enemies. His law may have been lost to you, and your heart may have formed many close alliances with foreigners. But a path is here opened before you, by which you may return, and which will lead you out of all that is contrary to his will. Don't be afraid to face the truth about your present spiritual condition; and don't admit the thought that you have been carried captive too far and too long for restoration to be possible. For in the swift transitions of our spiritual life, the very time that reveals a failure may reveal the remedy also, and at once that remedy may be applied and the soul delivered. That which took years for the children of Israel may be accomplished for you in a divine moment.

9   *There was a man in the land of Uz, whose name was Job; and that man was blameless and upright, one who feared God, and turned away from evil.* (Jb 1:1)

It was necessary that a righteous man should have been chosen to suffer what Job suffered, since it is the training of God's saints that is here set forth; and none but a good man could have understood the lessons or profited by them. Moreover it is plain to the simplest comprehension that a wicked man needs to be brought to the end of himself. But that an upright man should also need this is not so clear. Some Christians are mystified by the sufferings that beset them. It may be that they are conscious of the integrity of their hearts and cannot see the justice or the need for their trials. "I was doing what I thought right," such a Christian will say, "why should these things come upon me?" But the subtle forms of self-life that would ruin us, if left undiscovered and unchecked, are often most vigorous in those whose outward life is all that could be desired; and it needs sometimes a very sharp discipline to uproot them. In this fact lies hidden the secret of much that is mysterious in the dealings of the Lord with the souls of his servants. He loves us too much to permit any evil to linger undiscovered and uncured in our natures. This is not severity, but mercy. For the great object of all the discipline of life here is character-building. We are to be the "friends of God" throughout all eternity, and to be his *friends* means something far grander than merely being saved by him. It requires a far deeper harmony with his will. Therefore it is an unspeakable blessing that he loves us enough to take the necessary pains to make us fit companions for him. How well we know the strength of love it requires for us to discipline our children. Let us be thankful, then, that we have a God whose love is so strong that he will not withhold the hand of his discipline, until he has purged away all our dross, and taken away all our tin, and has presented us to himself a "glorious church, not having spot, or wrinkle, or any such thing."

10 *So Satan went forth from the presence of the Lord, and afflicted Job with loathsome sores from the sole of his foot to the crown of his head.* (Jb 2:7)

By all that happened to him, Job was brought to a knowledge of his own heart and was made to abhor himself in dust and ashes. The instrument used was Satan, but the hand that used this instrument was the Lord's. In both cases, when Job's possessions were taken, and also when his own body was smitten with sores, Satan's power extended only so far as the Lord permitted and not one hair's breadth further. While Satan seemed to do it all, there was One behind Satan, who overruled everything and made it all work together to accomplish his purposes of grace toward Job.

11   *Then Job answered: "Today also my complaint is bitter, / his hand is heavy in spite of my groaning." (Jb 23:1-2)*

When the Lord begins to empty us and to break us, the means he is obliged to use puzzle us and seem unreasonable, and often unkind and unjust. No chastening for the present *can* seem joyous to us but must necessarily be grievous, and we ought not to think it mysterious that it should be so. We must not question, therefore, nor admit the slightest inward rebellion against it, but thankfully submit to that which our Lord permits to come, let the instrumentality be what it may, whether Satan directly, or the wickedness and treachery of men. For not a sparrow falls without our Father's notice, and all that he permits to come upon us is meant to make us "partakers of his holiness," if only we will learn what he is trying to teach us. For it is the cross, and the cross alone, that brings us out of self.

Lives that we are apt to call wasted, which have ended in sorrow and humiliation, are not really wasted, but are simply being stripped of that which separated them from the Lord and from a perfect conformity to his likeness. That man is happy who goes into the next world emptied of self, no matter how painful the humbling may have been.

12 Job answered the Lord: / "Behold, I am of small account; / what shall I answer thee? / I lay my hand on my mouth. / I have spoken once, and I will not answer; / twice, but I will proceed no further." / Then the Lord answered Job out of the whirlwind. (Jb 40:3-6)

God took away all Job's possessions, everything in which he delighted or upon which he could rest; and then "out of the whirlwind," "out of the storm" he answered Job with a revelation of himself.

Just so is it sometimes now in the lives of God's children who have great possessions, whether inward or outward. Only "out of the storm" that has destroyed their possessions, can they have a revelation of God.

13 I had heard of thee by the hearing of the ear, / but now my eye sees thee; / therefore I despise myself, / and repent in dust and ashes. (Jb 42:5-6)

The moment came when Job could say from the depth of a convicted heart, "I despise myself, and repent in dust and ashes." But it did not come, until the Lord had revealed himself. That which all the reproaches and accusations of his friends had failed to do, one sight of God accomplished in a moment. Job had prayed that he might but see him and hear him speak, and the answer had come, bringing with it a revelation of self, which Job could hardly have expected, and yet which he found to be the beginning of richest blessings. He saw the Lord, but he also saw himself, as he was in the Lord's presence, and all his self-righteousness turned into filthy rags in an instant.

14 I have uttered what I did not understand, / things too wonderful for me, which I did not know. (Jb 42:3)

One deeply important lesson to be drawn from Job's experience is this, that all true knowledge of self and abhorrence of self must come, not from self-examination, but from beholding the

Lord. Until Job had his eyes opened to see the Lord, he was very well satisfied with himself, and all his self-examination seemed to lead only to self-justification. But the moment the Lord was revealed, all was changed, and the man, who, while looking at self had seen nothing but good, now despised himself in dust and ashes.

Self-examination is sometimes extolled among Christians as a most commendable and necessary duty; but in my view it is often a very great evil. It leads either to self-justification and self-commiseration, or else to discouragement and despair. It fills our lives with chapters full of the personal pronoun "I" and "my," as Job's was. The soul that looks away from self, and examines the Lord instead, finds its mouth filled with his name, and his praises, and his glorious power.

15 *And we all, with unveiled face, beholding the glory of the Lord, are being changed into his likeness from one degree of glory to another.* (2 Cor 3:18)

I feel very sure that the commands to look to Jesus, to behold his glory, to have our eyes ever toward the Lord, mean something very literal. And it is very certain that when we are looking to Jesus, we cannot see ourselves. For if our face is to the One, our back will necessarily be to the other. It is by "beholding the glory of the Lord" that we are to be "changed into his likeness." It is by keeping our eyes "ever toward the Lord," that our feet are to be plucked out of the net. It is by looking to him, that all the ends of the earth are to be saved.

Nothing hinders us more in our Christian life than to keep our eyes fixed on ourselves, trying to search out evidence of our own goodness and fitness for the mercy of the Lord, or tokens of our growth in grace. If we think we find any, then at once we are frightened at the danger of pride; and if we do not find any, then we are plunged into the depths of discouragement. The true way is to give up self as hopelessly bad and to have no eyes nor thoughts for anything but the Lord and his salvation. This, I think, is what the scriptures mean by self-denial and self-crucifixion. It is to say to this "I," "I am a stranger to you," and to refuse to listen for a moment to its pretensions or its claims.

16 *Awake to punish all the nations; / spare none of those who treacherously plot evil.* (Ps 59:5)

Besides those psalms which expressly refer to the Lord Jesus, there are many others whose praises, desires, hopes, and deliverances could have in him alone their truest realization. Only by seeing this, can we understand much of what is written in the Psalms. And only by understanding that the desires for vengeance upon enemies is to be interpreted as referring to Christ's great enemy, Satan, and all his host of evil spirits, and to the dreadful effects of sin in the hearts and lives of men, can we be relieved from the painful sense of vindictive cruelty that otherwise would oppress us. The Lord, who has told *us* to love our enemies, and to do good to them that hate us, could surely not do otherwise himself; and I cannot but feel that we must read of his wrath as being directed against the sin and not against the sinner, and his vengeance as being poured out upon the cruel Enemy, who carries captive his helpless flock, and not upon the poor flock, thus attacked and enslaved.

17 *For to me to live is Christ, and to die is gain.* (Phil 1:21)

A poor woman was once scoffed at by an infidel for supposing that she, in her weakness and ignorance, could ever travel over the long and weary road from earth to heaven. "Ah, master," she replied, "It is a very short road, and easily traveled. There are only three steps in it." "Three steps," he repeated scornfully, "and what are they?" The answer was a memorable one—"Out of self, into Christ, and into glory." If then to some of my readers the road to present peace and victory looks long and hard, let me assure you that it only needs but two of these steps to take you there. Out of self, and into Christ! That is all. That is enough for the deepest experiences and the richest blessings. The process that brings this about may be hard for flesh and blood, but the end is worth it all. And, although hard, it need not be long, for entire consecration and perfect faith will hasten every stage. *We* often are many years learning our lesson, because we are not able to bear rapid and severe strokes of the divine chastising hand. "Out of self" is a step to be taken by faith, but it is also a step to be taken actually and experimentally as well. And the Lord's part is to turn our faith into a reality, by his dealings with us, both inward and outward. The life of trust looks beautiful to us, and we long to live it, but we forget that something must be done first. No soul can trust utterly in the Lord who has anything of self left in which to trust, and we must therefore come out of the self-life entirely, before we can fully enter into the life hid with Christ in God. For it is utter weakness alone that can bring any soul to the point of utter trust. If our faith will but grasp it now, and if we will but let the Lord work as he pleases, without any shrinking or hindrance on our part, who can say by what rapid steps he may bring us out into this place of perfect peace, or how soon he may make the language of absolute trust our language also.

18 *Praise the Lord, O my soul! / I will praise the Lord as long as I live.* (Ps 146:1-2)

Let us join in this anthem here and now. Let us praise God whether we understand him or not. Let us praise him, even though his ways with us may seem to be too mysterious ever to be understood. Let us praise him out of our weakness, and out of our ignorance, and out of our very vileness itself. Let us praise him that we *are* weak, and ignorant, and covered with infirmity, because this is our most irresistible claim upon him, and because only so can his power rest upon us. Let us praise him that we are nothing and that he is all.

19 *All things have been delivered to me by my Father; and no one knows who the Son is except the Father, or who the Father is except the Son and any one to whom the Son chooses to reveal him.* (Lk 10:22)

We may, and we do, have all sorts of thoughts of God. We may conjecture this or imagine that, but we are wasting our energies in it all. We simply cannot know God. No man can, except through the revelation of Christ.

We may know a good many things *about* him, but that is very different from knowing him, as he really is in nature and character. Other witnesses have told us of his visible acts, but from these we often get very wrong impressions of his true character. No other witness but Christ can tell us of the real secrets of God's bosom. It will make all the difference in our Christian lives, whether or not we believe this to be a fact. If we do believe it to be a fact, then the stern judge and hard taskmaster whom we have feared, even while we tried to follow him, and whose service we have found so irksome and so full of discomfort, will disappear; and his place will be taken by the God of love who is revealed to us in "the face of Jesus Christ," the God who cares for us as he cares for the sparrows, and for the flowers of the field, and who tells us that he numbers even the hairs of our head.

20 *When he has brought out all his own, he goes before them, and the sheep follow him, for they know his voice.* (Jn 10:4)

Our Lord has declared that his sheep shall "know his voice," but we shall need to live very near him, and have much close communion with him before this can be. For amid the multitude of voices clamoring for our attention, it is not easy to distinguish the Shepherd's voice, unless we have become familiar with its sound. At first all voices are alike to the infant, and some time must pass before it can learn to distinguish even its mother's tones; and doubtless in the learning it makes many mistakes. But the time comes when the child knows that dear voice from every other and cannot mistake it, and when the voice of a stranger makes it afraid. And for us also, if we but follow on to know unwaveringly, the time will surely come when we likewise shall be able to distinguish the Shepherd's voice and shall "flee from the voice of a stranger."

21
The sheep hear his voice, and he calls his own sheep by name and leads them out. (Jn 10:3)

Not long ago a friend told me the following story. A farmer, wishing to purchase some sheep, made a selection from the flocks of a neighbor and started to drive them home. But he found it impossible to induce a single sheep to leave its owner's sheepfold by any force or persuasion. In despair he called upon the shepherd, who told him the trouble was that the sheep did not know his voice. Going to the fold himself, the shepherd stood and called them. Immediately, every one of the sheep bounded eagerly and joyfully out. He walked on, the sheep following him through strange and unknown roads, while he called out continually to let them know that he was their leader, until he had secured them safely in the sheepfolds of their new owner. No doubt these sheep would come to know the voice of their new shepherd, but, until they had learned it, they could not follow him willingly, nor yield a ready obedience to his commands.

Subjection to a voice is one of the sweetest ways of learning to know it. We shall find that each time we obey the voice of our Shepherd, it will become easier for us to distinguish it the next time.

22
Vanity of vanities, says the Preacher, / vanity of vanities! All is vanity. (Eccl 1:2)

It may seem sad to some that the world should be so unsatisfactory that "all is vanity." But when we understand the reason for it and the blessed result, we will surely praise the Lord with all our hearts that he has so arranged it. For he has commanded us to hate the world and to forsake it, and how could we obey him if it was attractive and satisfying? If there should be poison in our food, would we not be thankful if it had so bitter a taste as to make it impossible for us to eat? And, since there is a fatal poison in the world to all who love it, shall we not be thankful that the Lord has given it such a bitter taste as to make it too nauseous to be enjoyed for very long? If we understood this, we would not grieve so bitterly over the spoiling of our pleasant plans, or think it so mysterious that disappointments should come. For it is a grand victory not to love the world; and the soul that has gained this victory finds itself set in a large place, and cannot help but be thankful for whatever disappointment may have brought it there.

23 Which of you by being anxious can add one cubit to his span of life? And why are you anxious about clothing? Consider the lilies of the field, how they grow; they neither toil nor spin; yet I tell you, even Solomon in all his glory was not arrayed like one of these. (Mt 6:27-29)

The lily grows by the power of its inward life principle and according to the laws of a lily's life. No amount of its own stretching or straining, nor any pulling up by others, would help its growth. It is all folly and worse than folly, for Christians to make such mighty efforts to grow. If they would only let the Christ life within them grow, unhindered by their interference, they need have no fear of the result. But we are so ignorant of the laws of our spiritual life, that we are continually tempted to meddle with it.

Let us imagine a seed that has just been quickened, talking to itself. "What dreadful place am I in? How can anything grow in the dark like this, and with such heaps of heavy earth on top of it? And, oh dear! what is the matter with me? I seem to be all splitting up! Look at that bit of me going down! I thought I was meant to grow upwards. What does it all mean? I am afraid things are all wrong. Just when I thought I was getting out into the nice sunshine, here comes a dreadful storm and drenches me. I can never live through all this. Besides, look how little I am. I know I was meant to be a big tree. Where is the fruit I was to bear? I have only got two or three tiny green leaves." And so on, and so on.

Have you never known anyone who has made similar complaints?

24 *Well done, good and faithful servant; you have been faithful over a little, I will set you over much. (Mt 25:21)*

One evening in the spring of 1819 Thomas Moore wrote in his diary: "The sunset this evening was glorious; the thoughts that came over me while I looked at it, of how little I have done in the world, and how much my mind feels *capable of*, would have made me cry like a child if I had given way to them." The discrepancy between aspiration and achievement here expressed is a thing which has frequently been lamented. Most persons of any sensibility have at some time been troubled with a sense of it; yet, notwithstanding all the manifold regrets it has occasioned, nobody appears to be benefited by the contemplation of former failures, but every new adventurer in the pursuits of life repeats the old experience. It would seem as if the greater part of our existence were little more than an apprenticeship to the business of living; and that if ever we come to understand how our time and talents might have been most wisely employed, it is at a stage of life when the journey is drawing to a close, and hardly an opportunity is left us to turn what we have been learning to account.

It is impossible that anyone not wholly degraded and ignorant should be able to contemplate a nobler and better form of his own life without desiring in some measure to realize it. The very fact that it is nobler and better makes it desired. Everyone wishes to become the best he can be. The wish may not always be very effective, but still, the desire naturally springs up. This desire is what is termed "aspiration." To keep one's foot firmly set in the way that leads upwards is to conquer.

25 *For to you is born this day in the city of David a Savior, who is Christ the Lord. (Lk 2:11)*

If Christ is called by any one name more than another it is Savior. He is called over and over the Savior of the world. No one can question that this is his God-given name. He is one who saves. He is not one who merely offers to save, but he must of necessity, from the very nature of the name, be one who actually does it. The only claim to the name lies in the fact behind the name. We might as rightly call a man a king who had only offered to reign, as to call a man a savior who has only offered to save. When we say Christ is our Savior, what are we thinking of him? Do we think of him as One who is actually saving us now? Or do we think of him as One who only offers to save us at some future time, and who has accompanied that offer with such well-nigh impossible conditions that salvation is practically not available for us at all? Everything in our Christian life depends, not on what we say of Christ, but on what we think of him when we call him our Savior.

26 *A friend loves at all times.* (Prv 17:17)

Much of the happiness and purity of our lives depends upon our making a wise choice of our companions and friends. Friendship is based upon common sympathies arising out of oneness of tastes, sentiments, forms of thought and feeling, and modes of life. These common sympathies thus beget affection which makes intercourse a happiness. Friendship increases the range of life by making the interests, the aims, the affections of others as precious and dear to us as our own. It divides sorrows and multiplies joys. Each friend is another self. Not only does friendship thus widen the range of life by this simple process of adding the interests of others to our own and multiplying our sympathies by theirs; it raises our common life to a higher plane. It is the constant intercourse of friends, the gradual development of one another's thoughts and feelings, the reciprocal stimulus to intellectual action, the communication to one another of new truths, new interests, new projects—these things it is which constitute the happiness of social intercourse, and which can only take place truly and fully among real friends.

27 *For this is why I wrote, that I might test you and know whether you are obedient in everything.* (2 Cor 2:9)

Until you have found and obeyed God's will in reference to any subject as it is revealed in scripture, you need not ask nor expect a separate, direct, personal revelation. A great many fatal mistakes are made in this matter of guidance by overlooking this simple rule. Where our Father has written out for us a plain direction about anything, he will not of course make a special revelation to us about that thing. If we fail to search out and obey the scripture rule, where there is one, and look instead for an inward voice, we shall open ourselves to the deceptions of Satan and shall almost inevitably fall into error. No man, for instance, needs or could expect any direct revelation to tell him not to steal, because God has already in the scriptures plainly declared his will about it. This seems such an obvious thing that I would not speak of it, but that I have frequently met with Christians who have overlooked it and have gone off into fanaticism as the result. I know the Bible does not always give a rule for every particular course of action, and in these cases we need and must expect the direct voice of the Spirit.

28 *When a man vows a vow to the Lord, or swears an oath to bind himself by a pledge, he shall not break his word.* (Nm 30:2)

Because God is not visibly present to the eye, it is sometimes difficult to feel that a transaction with him is real. If, when we made our acts of consecration, we could actually see him present with us, we should feel it to be a very real thing, and would realize that we had given our word to him and would not dare to take it back, no matter how much we might wish to do so. Such a transaction would have the binding power that a spoken promise to an earthly friend always has to a man of honor. We need to realize that God's presence is a certain fact always, and that every act of our soul is done in his presence. A word spoken in prayer is really spoken to him as if our eyes could see him and our hands could touch him. Then we shall cease to have such vague conceptions of our relations with him, and shall feel the binding force of every word we say in his presence.

29 *According to your faith be it done unto you.* (Mt 9:29)

Try to imagine yourself acting in your daily life as you do in your spiritual life. Suppose you should begin tomorrow with the notion that you could not trust anybody, because you had no faith. When you sat down to breakfast you would say, "I cannot eat anything on this table, for I have no faith, and I cannot believe the cook has not put poison in the coffee, or that the butcher has not sent home a diseased piece of meat." You would starve to death.

When you went outside, you would say, "I cannot ride in a car for I have no faith, and therefore I cannot trust the driver, the factory that constructed the car, or the street signs." You would be forced to walk everywhere. Besides becoming weary with the effort, you wouldn't be able to reach all the places you could reach in a car. You would be forced to disbelieve many things, saying, "I really cannot believe there is any such person as the president or the Queen of England, for I never saw them, nor any such country as Ireland, for I was never there. And I have no faith, so of course, I cannot believe anything that I have not actually felt and touched myself."

Just picture a day like this, and see how disastrous it would be and what utter folly it would appear to anyone who watched you. Realize how your friends would feel insulted, and how your co-workers would refuse to work with you another day. Then ask yourself—if this lack of faith in other people would be so dreadful and such utter folly, what must it be when you tell God that you have no power to trust him nor to believe his word?

30 *When the Son of man comes, will he find faith on earth?* (Lk 18:8)

There are two things which are more utterly incompatible than even oil and water, and these two are trust and worry. Would you call it trust, if you gave something into the hands of a friend to attend to for you and then spent your days and nights in anxious thought and worry about it? Can you call it trust, when you have given the saving and keeping of your soul into the hands of the Lord, if day after day and night after night you are spending hours of anxious thought and questioning about the matter? When a believer really trusts anything, he ceases to worry about it. Worry only comes when trust is not present. Tested by this rule, how little real trust there is in the church of Christ. No wonder our Lord asked the pathetic question, "When the Son of man comes will he find faith on earth?" He will find plenty of activity and a great deal of earnestness, but will he find *faith*—the one thing he values more than all the rest? It is a solemn question, and every Christian heart should ponder it well.

31 *The end of the matter; all has been heard. Fear God, and keep his commandments; for this is the whole duty of man.* (Eccl 12:13)

All that is really necessary for life is declared to us in this one passage. The message of Ecclesiastes is that we cannot understand the world; we cannot find any comfort in it; it is all hopelessly empty and mysterious. But, even so, the Lord reigns and holds the clue; and to fear him and keep his commandments is the only thing needed to make everything straight. Obedience is the golden key to every mystery. Those who do his will shall sooner or later understand. A walk with him is a walk through a region of grandeur, and life is transfigured before us. Let us praise him, then, that the only thing which is declared to be our duty, is also the only thing possible for us to do. For the "world passes away, and the lust thereof: but he that does the will of God abides forever."

Scripture Index